THE H̶A̶M̶L̶Y̶N̶ LECTURES
FORTY-FIFTH SERIES

THE ADMINISTRATION
OF JUSTICE

AUSTRALIA
The Law Book Company
Brisbane – Sydney – Melbourne – Perth

CANADA
Carswell
Ottawa – Toronto – Calgary – Montreal – Vancouver

AGENTS
Steimatzky's Agency Ltd., Tel Aviv;
N.M. Tripathi (Private) Ltd., Bombay;
Eastern Law House (Private) Ltd., Calcutta;
M.P.P. House, Bangalore;
Universal Book Traders, Delhi;
Aditya Books, Delhi;
MacMillan Shuppan KK, Tokyo;
Pakistan Law House, Karachi, Lahore

THE ADMINISTRATION OF JUSTICE

by

The Rt. Hon. the LORD MACKAY OF CLASHFERN

Published under the auspices of

THE HAMLYN TRUST

LONDON
STEVENS & SONS/SWEET & MAXWELL
1994

Published in 1994 by
Stevens & Sons Limited/Sweet & Maxwell Limited of
South Quay Plaza
183 Marsh Wall
London E14 9FT
Phototypeset by
LBJ Enterprises Ltd. of Aldermaston
and Chilcompton
Printed in England by
Clays Ltd., St. Ives plc.

A CIP catalogue record for this book is
available from the British Library

ISBN 0-421-52250 X   (H/b)
ISBN 0-421-522607   (P/b)

Contents

The Hamlyn Lectures

The Hamlyn Trust

The Hamlyn Trust owes its existence to the will of the late Miss Emma Warburton Hamlyn of Torquay, who died in 1941 at the age of eighty. She came of an old and well-known Devon family. Her father, William Bussell Hamlyn, practiced in Torquay as a solicitor and JP for many years, and it seems likely that Miss Hamlyn founded the trust in his memory. Emma Hamlyn was a woman of strong character, intelligent and cultured, well-versed in literature, music and art, and a lover of her country. She travelled extensively in Europe and Egypt, and apparently took considerable interest in the law and ethnology of the countries and cultures that she visited. An account of Miss Hamlyn by Dr Chantal Stebbings of the University of Exeter may be found, under the title "The Hamlyn Legacy," in volume 42 of the published lectures.

Miss Hamlyn bequeathed the residue of her estate on trust in terms which it seems were her own. The wording was thought to be vague and the will was taken to the Chancery Division of the High Court, which in November 1948 approved a Scheme for the administration of the trust. Paragraph 3 of the Scheme, which closely follows Miss Hamlyn's own wording, is as follows:

"The object of the charity is the furtherance by lectures or otherwise among the Common People of the United Kingdom of Great Britain and Northern Ireland of the knowledge of the Comparative Jurisprudence and Ethnology of the Chief European countries including the United Kingdom, and the circumstances of the growth of such jurisprudence to the intent that the Common People of the United Kingdom may realise the privileges which in law and custom they enjoy in comparison with other European Peoples and realising and appreciating such privileges may recognise responsibilities and obligations attaching to them."

The Trustees are to include the Vice-Chancellor of the University of Exeter, representatives of the Universities of London, Leeds, Glasgow, Belfast and Wales and persons co-opted. At present there are eight Trustees:

Professor J.A. Andrews, M.A., B.C.L.
Professor T.C. Daintith, M.A.

From the outset it was decided that the Trust's objects could best be achieved by means of an annual course of public lectures of outstanding interest and quality by eminent Lecturers, and by their subsequent publication and distribution to a wider audience. Details of these Lectures are given on page vii. In recent years, however, the Trustees have expanded their activities by organising supplementary regional lecture tours and by setting up a "small grants" scheme to provide financial support for other activities designed to further public understanding of the law.

The forty-fifth series of lectures was delivered by The Right Honourable Lord Mackay of Clashfern, the Lord Chancellor, at the Institute of Advanced Legal Studies, London, in November 1993.

August 1994   **DESMOND GREER**
Chairman of the Trustees

1. The Judges

The object of the charity under which these lectures are given is the extension by lectures or otherwise of the knowledge of those referred to as "the common people of the United Kingdom of Great Britain and Northern Ireland" of the privileges which in law and custom they enjoy in comparison with other European peoples, so that as a result of such realisation they may appreciate their privileges and may recognise the responsibilities and obligations attaching to them. It is suggested that this object may be attained by furthering their knowledge of the comparative jurisprudence and ethnology of the chief European countries, including the United Kingdom. The particular part of our law and custom to which I wish to draw attention in my lectures is the administration of justice. As the purpose of the series already makes clear, I must not confine my attention to one part of the United Kingdom and I therefore have prominently in view that there are three distinct systems of administration of justice within the United Kingdom of Great Britain and Northern Ireland. By far the largest is that of England and Wales. Scotland has its own distinctive systems, both of substantive law and for the administration of justice. In Northern Ireland the substantive law is based on English common law, but it is affected by statutory provisions, many of which apply only in Northern Ireland, and it has its own distinct judiciary.

I propose to begin with a feature which is common to the three jurisdictions in the United Kingdom, namely the nature of the judiciary. In all three systems the judiciary is composed of individuals who have been appointed by or on behalf of Her Majesty The Queen from those who have practised the profession of the law otherwise than as judges

1

for a substantial proportion of their lives. We do not have a
judiciary which young people may enter at the beginning of
their careers and in which they may be promoted from one
level to another, possibly interspersed with periods of
service as a prosecutor on behalf of the State or as an
administrator or adviser in a Government Ministry or
Department. Such judges and judiciaries are often administered as a unit, with a subordinate judge being in some
form of line management in relation to a superior.

Our system selects judges from those who have been in
private practice in the profession generally. Considerable
emphasis is placed on experience of the courts. Accordingly
the principal, though not exclusive, qualification for judicial
office has been experience of advocacy for a certain minimum period. This period is laid down by statute in respect
of each of the offices in question. In practice, those
appointed have been persons who have attained a reputation for integrity of judgment and for learning and experience which has commanded the respect of the legal
profession. It is important that a judge should command in
his or her court the respect of those who appear in it to
practice before him. The judicial office, and the appointment by which it is conferred, gives authority. But the
personal standing of the office holder in the eyes of those
who practice in the court is an important complementary
support for that authority. Authority must be comple-
mented by respect. It is vitally important that the professional judiciary should be of high standing in the legal
profession with qualities of good judgment, humanity and
vision.

As I shall explain later, in England and Wales no-one is
appointed to full-time judicial office without serving for a
period in a part-time office. But these holders of part-time
office are dealing with real cases, of no less importance to
the people involved than cases heard by the full-time
judiciary. There is no question of a "mock" trial being the
subject of their work. They are appointed by or on behalf of
The Queen to administer justice between parties. It is
therefore essential that those who attain even the part-time

office have already the qualities which, at their level of entry into the judicial system, it is reasonable to expect.

The emphasis placed on advocacy in the qualifications to which I have referred arises from the practical necessity that those who preside over the court should be familiar with its working and be able to give authority to rulings as cases proceed without undue delay or hesitation on matters of evidence and procedure. This emphasis on experience in advocacy has, however, been challenged on occasion and I think it may well be that to rely wholly on advocacy practice gives undue weight to this factor. The pre-eminent qualities required of a judge are good sound judgment based upon knowledge of the law, a willingness to study all sides of an argument with an acceptable degree of openness, and an ability to reach a firm conclusion and to articulate clearly the reasons for the conclusion. Some who have not practised advocacy in the courts may well have these qualities to a great degree. They may have given sound advice both in contentious and non-contentious matters to clients over a considerable time. I believe that those who have these qualities may be able to acquaint themselves sufficiently with the procedures of the courts and the detailed rules of evidence in order to discharge the duties of a judge. It would not, therefore, be right to exclude them from consideration when a judicial office is to be filled.

A particular method by which this can be achieved is the promotion from one judicial office to another. In the lower rungs of the judicial ladder it may be easier to secure acquaintance with the procedure and rules of adjudication as cases proceed and this, at least, is one way in which a person who possesses the necessary judicial qualities may suitably move up to higher judicial office, after having gained experience of practice and procedure in a lower tribunal.

Part-time judicial positions - those at the bottom of the ladder - are much sought after. There is a considerably greater number of applicants than the training arrangements by which the applicants are inducted to their work can accommodate. Hitherto it has been the practice to take time to accumulate the necessary information about individuals and deal with their applications accordingly. For those who are seen as high fliers, the evidence often accumulates quickly; for those whose performance may be more standard it takes longer. When the necessary information is available to justify it, applicants are interviewed by a member of the staff of the Lord Chancellor's Department and a serving Recorder or judge or retired judge. From there, the progress up the judicial ladder will be in accordance with assessments which are forthcoming from the professional community. Under our present arrangements, these assessments are made by members of the Bar or judges who have some familiarity with the work of the part-time judges. These assessments are given in confidence.

This practice in England and Wales of requiring anyone seeking full time judicial office to serve first for a period in part-time judicial office has, then, as its main purpose the opportunity to judge how the candidate will perform as a judge, to test out whether the requisite qualities are present, and thus to reach a conclusion as between competing candidates for permanent judicial office who is the best fitted. I personally believe that this is an excellent method of selection since there is no better way of judging a person's qualification for a job than seeing how he or she performs in it.

However the requirement that a person should sit for a period as a part-time judge makes it difficult for those who practise law in at least some parts of the service of the state to be considered for full time judicial appointment. In particular if a person is employed by the Crown Prosecution Service in England, but aspires to judicial office, the requirement that he or she serve part-time for a period would, I think, necessarily require that employment in the Crown Prosecution Service should cease before the part-time work is embarked upon. It is generally necessary that the part-time work is spread over a period and obviously there is no guarantee when the person is first appointed part-time that he or she will succeed in obtaining a full-time appointment. In these circumstances it is difficult to see how the full range of people engaged in the courts in a legal practice can be considered for judicial office under this system.

In Scotland, on the other hand, it has not been required as a matter of practice that everyone aspiring to full time judicial office should first serve part-time. Procurators Fiscal, who are the prosecutors in their area representing the Lord Advocate, have, from time to time, been appointed to the Sheriff Court and I believe that many of them have been found very acceptable in this role. It is part of the tradition of the Procurator Fiscal Service, which has a long history in Scotland, that the holders of that office exercise a strong quasi-judicial independence in deciding whether or not a particular case should be prosecuted. Weighing the considerations which are required is an experience which may well provide a sound basis for the exercise of judicial office.

Another aspect which may merit comparison of the situation on the two sides of the Tweed is that, in England and Wales, prosecution in the Crown Court is done by Counsel who sometimes appear for the prosecution and sometimes appear for the defence. This gives a balance of experience which I regard as valuable for the central, independent and impartial role which the judge has to play. In Scotland, on the other hand, prosecution in the Sheriff Court is generally in the hands of a Procurator Fiscal and his qualified staff, and therefore in that court the private practitioner generally appears only for the defence. In the High Court in Scotland the prosecution is in the hands of the Lord Advocate and his Deputes, so that at any one time Counsel who is a Depute will be presenting no defence cases. However, the tenure of a Depute's office is fairly short, up to about three years, and accordingly any Counsel who appears in the High Court has an opportunity of doing so both for the prosecution and the defence if he has been appointed at some time an Advocate Depute.

My conclusion is that the different practices with which I am familiar have a useful part to play in the experience of those who are qualified for judicial office. The judicial temperament is an important feature of good advocacy at any level and for whatever party. I am sure that all who have experience as judges know how ineffective is the advocate who cannot distinguish a good point from a bad and takes them all with equal enthusiasm. On the other hand those who can judge which are good points, and put at least the primary emphasis on these, are well qualified. I have sometimes heard it said that good advocates can make bad judges and conversely. To some extent I believe that this is true. The gifts which are bestowed on human beings are in different combinations, and with different emphases. A person who has been given a superb talent as an advocate may not be so strong in judging whether the points he advocates are good or bad, if one is thinking of advocacy from the point of view of skill, eloquence and force in the presentation of a single point. On the other hand, as I have said, I believe that effective advocacy in a case depends not only on such skills but also on the judgment of which are good points or bad, and therefore I personally consider that effective advocacy does require a considerable measure of judgment.

Apart from the rather rare cases in which a person has been appointed from a position in an organisation such as the Procurator Fiscal Service, our judges have been recruited from private practice, in which each advocate practices on his own. To some extent this individuality may be tempered. Advocates generally work from chambers, with its supporting organisation; they will work from time to time as a junior to a leader or as the leader in a case and therefore as part of a team. But they will not be members of an organisation with responsibility to manage others - or with the experience of being managed themselves in a hierarchal system. This is an important characteristic of those who later in their careers may form part of our judiciary.

Our method of appointing judges has stood the test of time and is producing, I believe, a judiciary of a very high quality. All those who are concerned with comparative jurisprudence say that the standard of written judgments from the United Kingdom judiciary is generally very high. Judges deal in public with a very large number of cases. The proportion in which any sensible criticism has been made of the judge and of his discharge of his duties is very small. These are two independent indicators of the strength of our judiciary. Even if one takes full account of all that has been said about miscarriages of justice, in very few of the cases can legitimate criticism be levelled against the judges. The tribunal has been a jury and very often the cause of the subsequent setting aside of the conviction has been evidence, produced after the date on which the original proceedings were terminated, which cast doubt on the reliability of evidence that was before the jury. No doubt it is possible to take different views of some of these cases but, even if one takes the view most unfavourable to the judiciary, their number is still extremely small in comparison with the total number of cases heard.

Complaints have been made that there is no lay involvement in the selection of judges. I regard the selection of professional judges as essentially a matter on which the professional judgment is the more reliable, but I appreciate that the judges are appointed to serve the general public, not just the profession, and that accordingly the type of impression that an applicant makes on a lay person may well give a useful insight into his or her potential performance as a judge. Subject to considering how such lay people might be selected, I therefore think there is much to be said for incorporating a lay person in the interviewing panel.

If, as I believe is just, one accepts that the present standing of our judiciary is high, ought we to change the system? Various other systems operate in different parts of the world. Judges could be appointed after an election. I think the British people would not feel that this was a very satisfactory method of appointing the professional judiciary in our country, apart altogether from questions about the nature of the platform on which they would seek election, who would bear the cost of their running and for what term they should be elected.

An alternative is that there should be some form of Commission or Board which determined at least who was suitable for appointment and which might, in fact, also be the appointing body. I can see that if one were considering the establishment of a new system for the judiciary such a body might be regarded as appropriate. My own view is that it would lose at least one of the desirable features of the present system and might involve losing more.

I believe that the fact that the function of recommending/ making the appointment of the judiciary up to the level of the High Court falls to the Lord Chancellor alone[1] - and for the higher courts, both here and in Scotland, to the Prime Minister - secures individual personal responsibility for the propriety of the appointments and their success. This has proved extremely valuable over the years. The importance of these appointments and the nature of the tenure to which judges are appointed, has meant that those who have this responsibility have discharged it with a close, strong and personal interest and a feeling of immense responsibility. To diffuse that responsibility amongst a group, however well-qualified, would, I believe, lose an essential element of the system that has produced a judiciary of very high standing.

Second, the appointment by a Commission would either require an intimate knowledge by the members of the Commission of the candidates or involve the taking of references as well as the interviewing the candidates. I suspect that no-one who proposes such a Commission thinks of it as having an intimate knowledge of all possible candidates, or at any rate not in such a way that it could dispense with references and an interview. The more diffuse the circulation of references, the less likely they are to be frank and dependable. A Commission could well also breed different factions, each having a different approach to the type of judge required, with the possibility of splits along predictable lines. Finally, there is the problem that the Commission as a body could not be responsible to anyone, for questioning or for scrutiny of their methods. I therefore consider it preferable that the appointing or recommending authority should be one person directly accountable to Parliament, as in our system the Lord Chancellor and the Prime Minister are.

It has also been suggested that the nominations might be subject to approval, say, by a select committee of the House of Commons. I have carefully considered this suggestion,

---

[1] Lord Chancellor makes recommendations for appointments to the High Court and Circuit Bench appointments to The Queen. He makes a large number of other appointments, such as those of District Judges and to certain tribunals, himself.

since I can see that it might have some advantages. But I
believe that we do not appoint our judges for their opinions
but for the openness of their minds to consider questions
that may be put before them. The judicial role in our
system is to determine cases according to the evidence and
argument put in relation to the case, not according to
predispositions or previously held opinions which the judges
might have. Obviously every judge comes to a case with
previous experience and opinions formed in the light of that
experience. But the criterion for a good judge is, to my
mind, the extent to which he is able to apply his judgment
afresh to issues put before him and to relegate to the
background any such pre-formed views. The tendency of
prior examination, as one has observed in the United
States, is to discover and analyse the previous opinions of
the individual in detail. I question whether the standing of
the judiciary in our country, or the public's confidence in it,
would be enhanced by such an enquiry, or whether any
wider public interest would be served by it.

In discharging the responsibility of making or recommending judicial appointments, it is of the greatest importance that political views and affiliations are left out of
account. I can say for myself, and I hope it is generally
recognised to be a feature of appointments to the judiciary
by the Prime Minister or the Lord Chancellor, that considerations of that kind do not enter into the appointment of
judges in this country. It has been said that, because of their
background, education and so on, judges are often to be
regarded as belonging primarily to a particular political
point of view. If that was every true, I believe it is no longer
true today. Our judiciary comprise a broad range of independent and fair-minded people with a considerable variety
of attitudes and opinions.

Since the legal profession in this country is the base from
which our judiciary is recruited, it follows that those making
or recommending appointments are restricted by the nature
of the members of the profession available for appointment.
Over many years it had been difficult for women and
members of the ethnic minorities to reach the senior ranks
of the legal profession in the United Kingdom. This, I
believe, is in the course of changing, naturally and properly.

In the making of judicial appointments, every person who may be suitable should be taken into account. It is right to appoint the best person available at any particular time for the particular appointment. It is also right, in determining who that person might be, to take special account of the hurdles that individuals may have had to surmount in order to get to their present position in the profession. Circumstances of this kind should I think be taken into account, in doing all we can to retain the high quality of the judiciary by looking to the widest possible pool of well-qualified candidates.

In my account of the questions arising in relation to judicial appointments, I have so far spoken of the professional judiciary. But in England and Wales most criminal cases are adjudicated by lay magistrates. Here, qualifications in the law are by definition not required. But qualities of fairness, judicial temperament and willingness to hear both sides are as essential as in the professional judiciary. However, an additional factor arises. The lay magistracy is intended to be judging within a local community the members of that community, and it is important that the judged should see their judges as reasonably representative of the community to which they belong. For this reason, I do my best to secure (and the Chancellor of the Duchy of Lancaster does the same in the Duchy) people from all walks of life and from a broad mix of political affiliation, representative in a general way of the community in which they are called upon to dispense justice. The long history of the magistracy in England and Wales is a striking example of the public spiritedness of our citizens, their willingness to give of their time, their energy and their responsibility to the cause of justice. They play a vital role and everything possible should be done to encourage them in it.

One area in which it is suggested that it might be desirable to make some progress when considering reform of the judicial appointments system is the devising of criteria for selection procedures. In this I believe that it is instructive to look to selection procedures in comparable jurisdictions outside the United Kingdom. I hope that Miss Hamlyn will not mind too much if I look beyond Europe and to Commonwealth countries in doing so. The countries that I wish to consider are Australia, Canada and New Zealand.

A discussion paper, "Judicial Appointments," was published by the Attorney-General of Australia in September last.[2] The paper canvasses a range of options for change: criteria; advertisements; a judicial appointments commission. The paper suggests ten criteria for appointment. They are: legal skills; personal qualities; advocacy skills, practicality and common sense; vision (in the visionary rather than the 20/20 sense); oral and written communication skills; capability to uphold the rule of law and act in an independent manner; administrative skills and efficiency.

No criteria for appointment are published in New Zealand but there has been recent discussion to moving towards their formulation. Sir Geoffrey Palmer, formerly Attorney-General and Professor of Law at the Universities of Wellington and Iowa, has identified ten specific criteria: experience, knowledge of the law and professional skills, integrity, honesty and uprightness, industry, impartiality, appropriate age, good health, community experience and contacts, communication skills and collegiality. Sir Geoffrey rejects the concept of an appointments commission, and in doing so makes particular reference to the problems of accountability to Parliament.

At the Federal level in Canada and for senior appointments in the Provinces, the procedures for appointment of judges were changed in 1988. There are now committees consisting of politicians, judges, representatives of the legal profession and lay persons in each Province. These committees assess candidates as "highly qualified", "qualified" or "not qualified" on the basis of application forms and telephone consultations with colleagues. There are, however, no published criteria for appointment. The assessments made by the committees may be accepted or rejected by the Minister of State and I understand there is some criticism of the political and personal complexion of appointments.

[2] "Judicial Appointments - Procedure and Criteria"; a discussion paper by the Attorney-General of Australia, The Honourable Michael Lavarach MP, September 1993.

In some provinces in Canada, however, there are published criteria. These are too long to list here but relate to professional excellence, community awareness and personal characteristics. The Judicial Appointments Advisory Committee advertises specific vacancies, invites applicants to complete a 10 page application form, sifts applicants, makes discreet enquiries with judges and members of the legal profession, conducts interviews and ranks candidates. Of particular interest is the fact that the Committee keeps no record of their interviews or discussions in case these have to be made available under the Freedom of Information legislation. The Attorney-General, therefore, has only the application form, the Committee's ranking and a short paragraph of assessment prepared by the chair of the Committee on which to make his decision.

Several interesting points arise. The criteria devised by other jurisdictions do not appear to be related to any specific judicial office but attempt to summarise what is expected of a judge. This is interesting when comparing what we might consider, for the purposes of these lectures, to be the essential qualifications for judicial office. But it is not immediately obvious that all judicial offices require the same qualities. Second, the political influence is of concern in other countries. As I have said, I believe that this is not an issue here. Third, I would argue that the arrangements that exist in this country for the collection of data about candidates are comparatively well-developed and provide those who have to take the decisions with fuller information.

The independence of the judiciary is rightly regarded as a key principle of the constitution. I consider it to be absolutely vital to the health of a nation that the independence of the judiciary should be respected. What do I mean by the independence of the judiciary? I mean that every judge in deciding a case does so according to his own judgment, in the words of the judicial oath, "according to the laws and usages of this realm, without fear or favour, affection or ill-will". This means, among other things, that a judge deciding a case should do so without any influence being brought to bear upon him to decide it one way or another by any agency outside himself. It is often thought that the prime agency likely to influence a judge will be the executive government seeking to secure a judgment in its favour. It is of course vitally important that judges should be able to decide for and against the executive in all its branches according to the merits of the case without any influence whatever from the executive, except in the form of submissions put before the judge in accordance with the principles of natural justice with an opportunity for them to be countered by any opposing party.

However, judicial independence means more than that. It means that each judge, in giving judgment, is required to apply his own mind to the question before him and is not to be influenced by any other judge in an improper way. In a case in which the judge sits with other members of the court he is, of course, perfectly entitled to consider the views of the other members of the court in making up his own mind and if he thinks they are right, to follow them. On the other hand no other judge, however eminent, is entitled to tell one of his colleagues what to do. Such a direction is just as inappropriate as interference from any other outside agency, such as the executive. This does not mean that a judge sitting in a case will not take account of views expressed in other cases by his judicial brethren and, in particular, it does not mean that he will disregard judgments of a higher court which are binding upon him and which he is therefore duty bound to give effect in his court to the best of his ability. But it does mean that no judge is responsible in any way for the judicial work of another judge. A senior judge, the Lord Chief Justice for example, might give advice to a member of the Queen's Bench Division in respect of some aspect of a case appearing before him. But neither the Lord Chief Justice nor any other judge has a right to exert authority over the manner in which the judge performs the judicial function in the case before him.

The judicial independence to which I have referred above relates to the judge acting in court and delivering his judgments. Judicial independence, as I have said, is a key principle and must be preserved. Judges must be true to the judicial oath and no-one must be allowed to interfere with that. I doubt that anyone would disagree. But there can be differences of opinion on *when* the principle should apply. What constitutes a judicial decision; and what are the limits to which the principle can be invoked? Since judicial independence is so important and universally accepted as desirable it is a potent principle to invoke. But as with any principle - free speech, tolerance - care needs to be taken that it is not stretched to lengths that make it untenable. What is meant by judicial independence is a delicate and difficult area but one that I think is worth considering. I should say at once that I have come to no startling conclusion.

What constitutes a judicial decision? I doubt that any would argue that decisions on points of law or sentence, or in civil cases, on points of fact, delivered from the bench are not judicial decisions. One key feature is that they can be appealed - though this is not an infallible test; take for example judicial decisions of the House of Lords. At the other extreme are decisions or actions by judges off the bench about which it would be ridiculous to argue that judges should be free to act independently of any control - building without the necessary planning permission for example. In the middle, and they usually centre on the workings of the court, there are a range of decisions taken by judges that are less easy to categorise. In my next lecture, on the courts, I shall talk about the problems of listing cases. This is generally categorised as a judicial function. But it could be argued, though I should not wish to do so, that decisions on when cases should be heard is not fundamentally a judicial decision but an administrative one; and one on which considerations of importance to the executive should be brought to bear.

Similarly there are decisions taken by administrators and the executive that have a judicial flavour but which would not necessarily be categorised as judicial decisions. The first layer of decision making relating to entitlement to social security benefit, for example, though this can be appealed in certain circumstances, decisions on planning, on tax, on funding, on appointments - practically any decision in fact which brings two or more considerations together and on which a person not directly involved in the outcome has to decide. We would not expect the people taking these decisions to be able to invoke the principle of judicial independence. One reason for which I suspect we would not do so is because they are not people who are seen as judicial officers. In particular they have not been characterised as judicial officers taking any form of judicial oath.

To what circumstances beyond the restricted view of judicial decisions I described above is it reasonable to apply the principle? I shall refer later to the question of resources. But there is an argument that unless sufficient resources are provided the independence of the judiciary is circumscribed. Taken to its extreme, this must be right. If no resources are available - no courtrooms, staff, books, pay, not even a palm tree - then the judiciary would find it impossible to function and their independence would be as nought. But how far away from this scenario do you have to go before it becomes unrealistic to say that questions of resources are fettering the independence of the judiciary, or that it is justifiable to invoke the principle in arguing the case? I suspect that there are differing views on this point, just as there are differing views in the health service over clinical judgment, independence and the allocation of resources.

I raise these issues not because I wish to lead a dangerous life but because I do not wish to see the vital principle of judicial independence misused or devalued. Misused by being cited in situations for which it is not appropriate; and devalued by too widespread an application. If we are to safeguard the principle then we must be sure that it is applied only in circumstances to which it can properly be applied.

The principle of judicial independence has profound importance for the way in which views of and from the judiciary may be obtained. In a managed organisation such as the civil service, a senior officer has responsibility for managing the work of those working to him and one aspect of this is the responsibility to report upon the quality of their work and their suitability for undertaking different work or for promotion. As befits modern management practice, it is usual for the report written by the senior officer to be made available to the person on whom he is reporting. The junior may then discuss it, not with the reporting officer but with the reporting officer's own line manager. This ensures some degree of objectivity. The junior may wish to comment on the report. Such comments may be in writing, and before the report becomes final he or she is usually required to sign the report as evidence of this fact. Such is the ingratitude of human nature that the junior is less likely to thank the reporting officer for an unfavourable report than for a glowing one. Since most people like to be liked, the tendency in most managers might be to try to please and therefore to give a good report. But the other side of this is that, in a managed structure, if the report on the junior is undeservedly favourable, the reporting officer may find himself marked down for poor reporting in his own report. And equally if the glowing report is acted upon and the junior turns out not to be suitable for the work assigned to him or her, the judgment of the manager making the report will be found to have been unsound, with possible implications for the prospects of his career in the structure.

No such considerations apply in the judiciary. There is no basis upon which the Lord Chancellor or anyone else can require a judge to report upon another, or to offer appraisal or any other qualitative assessment of the judge's performance as a judge. This means that in so far as judges are prepared to comment on one another, or on prospective applicants for judicial appointment, they do so voluntarily on conditions which they find acceptable. The minimum acceptable generally is that the comments are confidential. This obviously limits the extent to which they can be used to inform those commented upon.

However, the other aspect of judicial work is that the vast majority of cases that come before judges are heard in open court, and their judgments are given publicly. In this way each judge is continuously before the public. The extent to which their judgments are scrutinised by the public depends a good deal on the subject matter of the judgments. We are all familiar with that small body of oft repeated quotations from judges which deal with matters of sex and rape. We are not so familiar with quotations from the judgments of members of the Commercial Court on the question of whether an action in this country should be stayed to allow the subject matter to be decided in a case in another country. Recently some journals have taken an interest in the success rate of appeals against judges and have used this as a method of appraisal. All of the facts relating to these matters are in the public domain and capable of being ascertained. It is possible to obtain the transcript of any case in the higher courts, although proceedings of the Appellate Committee of the House of Lords are not usually recorded verbatim. There is thus plenty of material in the public domain on the basis of which the judicial performance of a judge can be evaluated.

There is one judge on whom appraisal of a somewhat different kind bears rather heavily. A judge who can be removed by the Prime Minister at a moment's notice or - whilst not at a moment's notice, then as long as it takes to decide a general election - by the electorate. A judge with executive responsibilities which attract a certain amount of appraisal from Parliament, the press, the public and his fellow judges. The Lord Chancellor - for it is he - is responsible for the administration of justice and is the United Kingdom's most senior judge. Given the title of this lecture series I feel bound to indulge now in a little self-dissection.

In England and Wales, the responsibility for providing the resources for the administration of justice in terms of money, buildings, and staff lies with the Lord Chancellor in respect of the national courts although by statute this power is usually exercised with the consent of the Treasury. The same is true in Northern Ireland, while in Scotland that responsibility rests with the Secretary of State and is discharged through the Scottish Courts Administration. It has been questioned in recent times whether the arrangements in England and Wales and Northern Ireland are the best available. The Lord Chancellor is, by statute, President of the Supreme Court of England and Wales, he has responsibility for the County Court and he is entitled to preside if he sits on appeals in the House of Lords. With a judicial background, the Lord Chancellor should be well fitted to understand the problems associated with resources for the administration of justice and of the overlap and borderline between the responsibilities of the judiciary in this area and those of the executive. The Lord Chancellor's position as Speaker of the House of Lords and a member of the Cabinet gives him a voice both in the legislature and the executive which enables the claims of the administration of justice to be clearly articulated, particularly in the Cabinet and its committees.

On the other hand, where restrictions in the interests of restraint on public expenditure are seen to apply to the administration of justice, there is inevitable tension between his role as a judge and his role as a member of the executive. Since in practice no element of the Public Service ever gets as much resources as it would wish, such a tension between those who work in the Service and the executive Government as paymaster for the Service is inevitable. Is this tension so far as the administration of justice is concerned, better to be within an individual, the Lord Chancellor fulfilling both roles, or between the judiciary on the one hand and a Minister, not part of the judiciary, on the other? I believe personally that, painful as this tension can be for the individual who is Lord Chancellor, the fact that he is a member of the House of Lords who has no political ambitions for himself, that he is a senior member of the Cabinet respected there as a judge, and able to present the claims of the administration of justice with a considerable depth of knowledge, puts justice and the judiciary in a reasonably good position to obtain the necessary resources. But the fact that the head of the judiciary is also a member of the Cabinet does not mean that he can just present demands to the Cabinet for resources and expect them to be met without careful argument in support of them. The fact that the executive and judiciary meet in the person of the Lord Chancellor should symbolise what I believe is necessary for the administration of justice in a country like ours, namely a realisation that both the judiciary and the executive are parts of the total government of the country with functions which are distinct but which must work together in a proper relationship if the country is to be properly governed. The ultimate embodiment of this important concept is Her Majesty, with Her Majesty's Courts, Her Majesty's Government and Her Majesty in Parliament giving Her Royal Assent to Acts of Parliament, as Head of all these parts of Government.

I personally regard it as one of the Lord Chancellor's responsibilities to do his utmost to secure that this relationship works well and that any irritants in the system are resolved. It is also a feature of our system that the Lord Chancellor holds regular meetings with the other Heads of the Divisions of the Supreme Court and the Senior Presiding Judge. During the law terms, these meetings are held about once a month and are attended by the Lord Chief Justice, the Master of the Rolls, the President of the Family Division, the Vice-Chancellor and the Senior Presiding Judge, with such officials from the Lord Chancellor's Department as I consider appropriate for the particular business in hand. The Senior Presiding Judge provides a link between this meeting and the Presiding Judges for the circuits. These meetings are concerned with every aspect of the justice system. For example, one such meeting annually is always concerned with the appointment of new Queen's Counsel. Changes in the procedure for the appointment of judges, relationships with the media and all the current topics of interest in relation to the justice system figure from time to time in our discussions. Perhaps most recently and topically, we have discussed court dress. You will by now know the outcome.[3]

When it comes to provision of the resources, it is clear that the executive Government has the primary role to perform. The House of Commons is responsible for voting supply and in our system the estimates for supply voted by the House of Commons are proposed by the Government of the day. The decision of how much supply to raise and its allocation between the various parts of the Public Service is a matter for the executive Government to determine, subject to the approval of the House of Commons.

So far as the judges are concerned, their terms of service and remuneration are subject to provisions of primary legislation and their remuneration is charged on the Consolidated Fund. It is the responsibility of the executive Government to determine the level of judicial salaries but statute prevents these salaries from being lowered. The

---

[3] It was announced on September 30, 1993 that there was to be no change in court dress.

question in practice is whether and to what extent they should be raised from time to time. In recent years the arrangements have been that a review body makes recommendations to the Prime Minister, and the Government decides the extent to which those recommendations can be implemented in the economic circumstances of the time. So far as the rest of the money voted where the courts are concerned, it requires to be administered.

In many countries, including I think all the continental countries, this administration is the responsibility of a Ministry of Justice which usually, in many of the continental countries, also has important responsibilities in relation to the judiciary. Here, this responsibility rests with the Lord Chancellor. Before considering whether or not that is a good thing I should like to say a little more about what is involved. Like every prudent organisation seeking to raise funds, the Government proceeds on the basis of estimates of what may be required. Although a critically important estimate is that for the first year, the demands of longer term planning make it wise to plan for a three-year cycle of public expenditure. Each year, the provisional conclusions for years two and three of the former cycle will be reconsidered in the next. One of the problems of the justice system, which it shares with many other parts of the Public Service, is the difficulty of providing accurate estimates in advance of what may be required, because the factors influencing the requirements of the justice system are varied and very sensitive to changes in policy and human behaviour. Naturally, in the present climate, there is a considerable competition for funds between the various parts of the Public Service. The Government as a whole has concluded, with the support of the electorate, that public expenditure requires to be closely controlled so that the burden of taxation, with its inhibiting effect on the competitive position of this country and its industries, should be kept to a minimum. The system for controlling public expenditure has recently been altered to provide that an overall or planning total is agreed first, and this total is then divided amongst the various services. This involves a competition between spending ministries even more intense than in the past, where each Ministry negotiated with the

Treasury and the results of these negotiations were added up at their conclusion to find the total of public expenditure. Where the desire is to limit public expenditure, I have no doubt that the new method is the more effective, although the problem it creates for those with responsibility for administering the Public Service is greater.

Making estimates for the current year and the two years following is difficult but more is required. For example, in provision for the courts it is necessary to consider the provision of new buildings. There are many factors that call for a court building programme. We have in this country many fine courtrooms in buildings of distinction, well sited in the centres of towns and cities. It may be a reflection on attitudes to justice in the past, but many of these, notwithstanding their splendour, have very inadequate facilities for witnesses or jurors. In many it is extremely difficult to make separate provision for victims and for children, and there are frequent difficulties with access for the disabled and other services. Another factor is important in this connection. One of the daily tasks facing the courts is to try and ensure that listed cases start at the time for which they are listed. Because of the differences between cases, and the possibility of settlement or plea, there is great virtue in having a number of courts and judges sitting in the same building. The larger the assembly of courts, the more likely it is that the average behaviour of cases will apply in that court on any given day. Thus in relation to the convenience of witnesses and jurors, there is much to be said for assembling a good number of courtrooms together.

On the other hand, the greater concentration of courtrooms, the less dispersed throughout the country the courthouses are. Although to be without a court altogether is probably an indication that a community is peaceful and law abiding, in my experience most communities regard it as a serious loss if a local courtroom is closed, and of course this is particularly true if the courtroom is a fine example of the type I have mentioned. Deciding the future pattern of a court building programme is therefore delicate and fraught with a number of political questions. Future patterns of crime as well as future population patterns must also be forecast in making these decisions, as courts built now will be expected to serve for a long period, and any individual investment is likely to be quite large. The failure to build an adequate number of courts today, or to plan for them, may well not be apparent nor produce detrimental results for some considerable time to come. So there is inevitable pressure, where a total vote is concerned, to use the available money to meet the exigencies of the moment at the expense of, for example, the court building programme.

When it comes to running costs and costs for maintenance, the various branches of the Public Service are anxious to obtain as much as possible, and the administration of justice is no exception. In this connection, it is obvious that decisions of judges can have a great effect on the use of resources. For example, if a trial has been going on for a considerable time, using court facilities, hearing witnesses, retaining jurors etc., and the judge concludes that something has gone wrong, possibly with the presentation of the prosecution case or a suggestion of interference with jurors, he has to consider whether to abort the trial. This must have substantial financial consequences. If the judge decides that a case is to be transferred to another court for reasons of possible prejudice, this too can have substantial repercussions in financial terms for the Court Service and for other agencies involved in the justice system. This illustrates that important decisions affecting the financing of the courts require to be taken by judges in the proper exercise of their judicial office without improper pressure from the executive.

The conclusion I draw from this is that, as in other Public Services, there is an overlap between the responsibilities of the central figures who provide this Service, in this case the judges, and the executive Government which finances the Service and raises the necessary taxation. My view is that it is unlikely to be of assistance in meeting problems of this kind associated with the justice system for the Head of the Judiciary to be removed from Executive Government. It seems more likely that the interests of the judiciary in matters within the concerns covered by the Treasury are more likely to be advanced if they can be pursued within government by a person with a lifetime of work in law and an understanding of the needs and concerns of the judiciary and who has responsibility as Head of the Judiciary, than if they were to be left within government as the responsibility of a minister with no such connection with the judiciary. Generally those who advocate fundamental change in the role of the Lord Chancellor do so with a view to increasing the accountability of the courts to the House of Commons. I believe that recent developments, particularly the appointment of a Parliamentary Secretary to the Lord Chancellor in the House of Commons[4] and the enlargement of the scope of the Home Affairs Select Committee of the House of Commons to include review of the work of the Lord Chancellor's Departments[5] together with the long established scrutiny of the Lord Chancellor's Department by the Public Accounts Committee of the House of Commons adequately secure these aims.

On this aspect I conclude that our historical development has produced a position for the independence of the judiciary with many indirect advantages which can develop further but which ultimately is sound.

Another aspect of the administration of justice which calls for mention in relation to the position of the Lord Chancellor is the appellate jurisdiction of the House of Lords and the Judicial Committee of the Privy Council, in both of which the Lord Chancellor is entitled to sit and preside. It is in these courts that the Lord Chancellor normally sits as a judge when he is in a position to do so. There are obvious restrictions on the cases in which it is appropriate for any judge to sit, although these are more general in the case of the Lord Chancellor than those which would ordinarily affect a judge. The Lord Chancellor would not sit in a case involving decisions of his own nor of members of the Government in their executive capacity. He can, however, sit on cases involving the construction of statutes passed by Parliament, possibly quite recently, and those concerning the interests of individuals or companies other than the Government.

It has also been customary for the Lord Chancellor to sit in cases involving important questions of law, even if

[4] On April 15, 1992.

[5] On July 18, 1991.

Government agencies are involved, where the decisions are not those of Ministers but of independent persons appointed for that purpose. The most notable of these as a litigant is the Board of Inland Revenue. That Board decides the application of the tax law to individual cases and is completely free from any influence of Ministers in such decisions. Similarly prosecution decisions are taken independently of the Cabinet and therefore again the Lord Chancellor has been in the habit of sitting from time to time in criminal cases. I believe that it is extremely important that the person with responsibility for administering the important boundary between the executive and the judiciary should have judicial experience and the opportunity to set judicially where the arrangements so permit. It is another important feature of the administration of justice in this country that any judge at whatever level has free access to the Lord Chancellor whenever he or she so requests and I endeavour to meet such requests as speedily as possible.

This brings me to an important question relating to the accountability of the judiciary. The Master of the Rolls recently gave an excellent address on judicial ethics[6] with which I very much agree, although as an independent judge he did not consult me in advance. He pointed out there are no disciplinary arrangements for judges of the High Court save that, under the Act of Settlement of 1702, they may be removed from office on a resolution to that effect by both Houses of Parliament. I am happy to say that no English judge has ever been removed in this way.

On the other hand the Lord Chancellor does have power to dismiss Circuit Judges and others. There is no formal arrangement for administering such discipline and I have never yet had to resort to dismissing a judge, although I have had occasion to consider whether it was my duty to do so. The paramount importance of maintaining the independence of the judiciary makes it necessary that this power should be used only very sparingly. Hitherto, and long may this continue, the judges could not with any degree of

[6] "Judicial Ethics", address by the Right Honourable the Master of the Rolls to the Society of the Public Teachers of Law, September 8, 1993.

plausibility be accused of misbehaviour. In this connection I sometimes receive complaints about conduct in court. In many cases, where the conduct has taken place in open court, independent evidence is available about what happened and indeed in some complaints the allegation is that words used in judgment were inappropriate for one reason or another. Sometimes I have complaints about hearings where there is little independent evidence available, but on the whole I think the judges' remarks in court have been reasonable except in those, principally criminal, cases which have received attention in the media. As the Court of Appeal has recently said, many of these criticisms are directed to judicial remarks torn out of their context.[7] I strongly feel that the media have a responsibility, in their criticism of judges, to give some attention to the context in which the judge speaks, and if they wish to be fair, to notice not only the remarks which they wish to criticise but also any surrounding remarks which might tend to mitigate the severity of their criticism. The idea that attacks on the judiciary by the press is a new development is, of course, ill-founded, but I think the coverage that some of these attacks get has become considerably greater. The ordinary members of the public to whom these lectures are directed would, I think, be wise to muse upon whether it is right that judges who are seeking to do their duty, often in difficult circumstances, should be subject to such abuse on the basis of a chance remark which, taken out of context, can appear absurd. The pressures under which judges work these days are certainly very high. If the public value the administration of justice in this country, they will wish to ensure that the judges carrying out their work diligently and responsibly are given appropriate public support.

Finally in this connection I should like to mention the matter of judges contributing to public discussion. The system under which judges were required to seek the consent of the Lord Chancellor before taking part in such discussion seemed to me difficult to reconcile with the independence of the judiciary and I indicated shortly after

[7] *R. v. Gambrill*, Court of Appeal, Criminal Division, July 29, 1993.

taking office that I would not require judges to seek my consent for such interventions.[8] I believe that those who have been given Her Majesty's Commission for the discharge of judicial office should have the judgment to decide such matters for themselves. There are many aspects to be considered and I and my colleagues are always willing to offer advice in particular situations but the change and the only change of substance I made was to place the responsibility to decide whether to intervene in public discussion on the shoulders of the judge concerned. Surely this is right.

In considering the administration of justice, it is right, as I said earlier, to consider the related public services and the Lord Chancellor's position in relation to them. The Lord Chancellor has responsibility for those portions of the civil law which are not the responsibility of any other Department, and for the administration of justice and the law relating to the courts. Until recently the Home Secretary had responsibility for the law relating to the magistrates' courts and central Government responsibility in relation to their administration. The magistrates' courts being a local justice service, their administration is local, but 80 per cent of the funding comes from central Government, which therefore has a central interest. This has now been transferred to the Lord Chancellor. He is therefore the Minister with responsibility for all courts, in so far as there is Ministerial responsibility for them. He is also responsible for an ever-growing number of tribunals although some are still the responsibility of other Ministries. For the policy of the criminal law and the procedure of the criminal courts, the responsibility rests with the Home Secretary. It is sometimes suggested that this division of responsibilities is confusing, but I regard it as important that the Lord Chancellor should not have this responsibility for criminal matters, which are very much matters for discussion in the House of Commons. I believe that the success of the office of the Lord Chancellor has depended to some extent on proper limitation of his role. The historical development of the Lord Chancellor's office is important in justifying its present existence. However its continued existence depends

[8] November 1987.

in my opinion on the Lord Chancellor being confined in policy terms to matters which are closely related to, and are compatible with, his responsibilities in relation to the administration of justice.

The inclusion of the Lord Chancellor in my consideration of the judges may surprise some and I am conscious that I am now straying further and further away in this lecture from the strictly judicial functions of this office. I have tried in this lecture to produce some insight into some of the themes that I believe are relevant at the moment to the judiciary and in this I certainly include its head, the Lord Chancellor. However I cannot hope to cover all aspects of matters relevant to the judiciary and I am sorry if I have not dwelt on areas that some might have been expecting from my title. My focus will shift to the courts and their administration in my next lecture and I will, of course, make some reference to the judiciary in that regard. I say this by way of encouragement to any wishing to hear more on the subject so that they may be able to attend next week.

2. The Courts

In the first of these lectures I began by remarking on a circumstance which applies in all three law districts of the United Kingdom, namely that the judges are drawn from the ranks of those who practise in the legal profession. In this lecture I shall draw attention to significant differences between the law districts in respect of the court structure.

So far as England and Wales is concerned, in criminal matters there is a wide jurisdiction presided over by magistrates appointed by the Lord Chancellor or, in the Duchy of Lancaster, by the Chancellor of the Duchy. There are around 29,000 magistrates. Nearly all of them are lay persons. There are also a small number, by comparison, of legally qualified magistrates who are referred to as stipendiary magistrates. I may say in passing that this is not a particularly happy description, although it is one of long standing and I think it draws attention to a distinction between the lay magistrates and their professional colleagues. I would say that it is, in fact, the least noteworthy of the distinctions between them. The fundamental distinction is that stipendiary magistrates are required to be qualified lawyers, whereas the remainder of the magistrates are not.

The vast majority of criminal cases are dealt with by magistrates' courts. The distinction between the courts on this aspect is provided in the definition of the offence in question - a summary offence being triable only in the magistrates' court; an offence on indictment being triable only in the Crown Court; and as the name implies, either way offences being triable in the magistrates' court or the Crown Court.

The next rung in the hierarchy of criminal courts is the Crown Court which was created by statute in 1971 and superseded the previous system. The judges of the Crown Court are all full time professional judges, save for those who sit as Recorders and Assistant Recorders. To save time I shall restrict my references to judges to the full-time judiciary. They comprise High Court judges and circuit judges who sit in the Crown Court. The High Court judges are mainly from the Queen's Bench Division, although Family Division judges also sit from time to time trying criminal cases in the Crown Court. The Crown Court deals with appeals from magistrates' courts and also has a trial jurisdiction for indictable only cases and cases which are triable either way. Appeal from the Crown Court in cases originally dealt with there lies to the Court of Appeal (Criminal Division). From that court there is only an extremely limited appeal to the House of Lords.

On the civil side, the magistrates' courts have civil jurisdiction to a rather limited extent but it includes family jurisdiction. The County Court is the local court for dealing with the less important civil cases, although its jurisdiction has been extensively developed as a result of the Civil Justice Review and the provisions of Part 1 of the Courts and Legal Services Act 1990. Its judges are all professional judges. They include the district judges, known formerly as registrars, and circuit judges. The High Court of Justice is the supreme civil court of original jurisdiction and is divided into three divisions - Queens' Bench Division, presided over by the Lord Chief Justice; the Family Division, presided over by the President of the Family Division; and the Chancery Division, presided over by the Lord Chancellor but in practice that aspect of the Lord Chancellor's functions is performed by the Vice-Chancellor who is the Head of Division with responsibility for the day to day administration of the Chancery Division. From the High Court as well as from the County Court there are rights of appeal to the Civil Division of the Court of Appeal, presided over by the Master of the Rolls. From the Civil Division of the Court of Appeal there is again a limited opportunity to appeal to the House of Lords.

In addition to these courts, a large number of tribunals have developed in the course of the present century. Many of these have jurisdictions relating to the areas in which particular Secretaries of State or other Cabinet Ministers have policy responsibility and there is a variety of arrangement for their administration. In more recent times the administration of the more senior of these tribunals has to some extent been made the responsibility of the Lord Chancellor, although this is by no means always the case. For example, the Employment Appeal Tribunal remains within the administrative responsibility of the Secretary of State for Employment. But the judges who serve in it are provided by arrangement with the Lord Chancellor (although in practice these arrangements are handled on a day to day basis by the Heads of Division) and the President of the Tribunal is appointed by the Lord Chancellor.

The position of the House of Lords as an Appellate Tribunal is an interesting phenomenon. The present arrangements have developed out of a situation in which appeals to the House of Lords originally were dealt with largely by the Lord Chancellor. There are now ten full-time Lords of Appeal in Ordinary and any member of the House who holds or has held high judicial office is qualified to participate in such appeals. General speaking the House delegates appeals coming to it to an Appellate Committee consisting of five Law Lords. In some circumstances where review of previous authorities or other factors makes the case one of particular importance, seven or more Law Lords may sit. It is interesting that whereas all Peers take an oath of allegiance at the start of a Parliamentary session, those who sit as Lords of Appeal, or Lords of Appeal in Ordinary as they are more properly known, do not take any judicial oath in respect of that office. The Lord Chancellor takes the judicial oath in the Royal Courts of Justice soon after he is initiated in his office by being presented by Her Majesty with the Great Seal and therefore he is the only judicial member of the House of Lords who takes a judicial oath in relation to sitting as a judge of the House of Lords. You may be interested to know that this has led to some question whether on being entertained by the Lord Mayor and the City of London at the Mansion House, the Lords of Appeal in Ordinary should stand or sit when the toast is proposed to Her Majesty's judges.

The Scottish system of courts is different in a number of important respects from those in England. First of all the distinction of the Scottish system is preserved by the Treaty of Union. It is one of the features of the legal system in Scotland which has remained comparatively untouched by United Kingdom legislation since the union, although of course there have been a number of Acts applying to Scotland which have made changes in the system of Scottish courts. Although in Scotland there is a district court at which Justices of the Peace and stipendiary magistrates sit, it is comparatively small in scope and certainly deals with a far smaller proportion of cases than does the magistrates' courts in England and Wales. The basic court in Scotland for both civil and criminal cases is the Sheriff Court. The Sheriff Court of a Sheriffdom is presided over by a Sheriff Principal, who is responsible for the administration of the courts in his Sheriffdom. The judges in the court are the Sheriffs - advocates or solicitors of substantial experience before appointment. They do the vast bulk of the work. The precise nature of what the Sheriff Principal does in the first instance work is a matter for his discretion but he also hears appeals in civil cases from the sheriffs. This is a comparatively unique appeal from a single judge to another single judge but it has considerable advantages in expedition and cost as well as flexibility in the venue in which the appeal is heard. The Sheriff Principal may often find it convenient to travel to the place in which the case was first heard in order to take the appeal. In addition there are temporary sheriffs who are appointed by Her Majesty and may be assigned to any sheriffdom temporarily to help where additional assistance is required. There are also honorary sheriffs commissioned by the Sheriff Principal who are lay people and who may be called upon from time to time to take courts in which comparatively straightforward business will be conducted.

The Sheriff Court is, as I have said, a court of civil and criminal jurisdiction. In its criminal jurisdiction it can operate in two different ways. First of all the Sheriff may sit alone to try cases summarily, in which event he is the judge on both fact and law. His powers of punishment are limited and this will in most cases determine whether or not a case is taken summarily before him. Statutory provisions may also determine that a particular statutory offence is to be tried summarily. The Sheriff may also sit as a presiding judge in solemn procedure with a jury of 15, where his powers of punishment extend to three years' imprisonment. On the civil side the Sheriff Court is a court of general jurisdiction and apart from some particular cases reserved to the Court of Session, any claim may be raised in it. There are powers of transfer in civil matters upwards and downwards between the Sheriff Court and the Court of Session.

The Supreme criminal court of Scotland is the High Court of Justiciary. As a court of trial the procedure in the High Court of Justiciary is solemn, that is to say a judge sits with a jury of 15 to try persons accused on indictment of more serious offences than would normally be taken in the Sheriff Court. The High Court goes on circuit and in recent times it has sat almost continuously in Glasgow and regularly in a number of other cities and towns in Scotland.

It is an interesting feature of the Scottish system that the prosecution determine the court in which particular criminal proceedings are taken. Prosecution is the responsibility of the Lord Advocate and his Deputes, the Solicitor General for Scotland and a number of members of the Bar entitled to practise in the Supreme Court with the Procurators Fiscal, the representatives of the Lord Advocate in the Sheriff Courts and the District Courts. This is an important aspect of the responsibility committed to the prosecution in Scotland which so far as I can judge has generally been discharged to the satisfaction of the public. I can remember only one or two cases in which any objection had been taken to the level of court to which a case had been sent. Of course, the Procurator Fiscal system in Scotland has a very long history and strong tradition; in particular it pre-dates the police service by a very long period.

On the civil side the Supreme Court of Scotland is the Court of Session. The Court of Session is a court of first instance with a very general jurisdiction, subject to some statutory exceptions in civil matters. The Court of Session is a collegiate court and until very recently it consisted of the Lord President and the Lord Justice Clerk and other judges all of whom are in exactly the same rank and with the same remuneration. When sitting at first instance the court normally consists of a judge sitting alone, although in exceptional circumstances he may sit with a jury of twelve. Appeal within the court from a judge sitting alone is to a division. Because of the geographical arrangements of the court in former times, the judge sitting alone is spoken of as sitting in the Outer House. Appeals are heard in the Inner House by a division of the court and this is usually presided over either by the Lord President or the Lord Justice Clerk - the Lord President in the first division, the Lord Justice Clerk in the second division. In exceptional circumstances there may be an extra division presided over by one of the other judges usually of considerable seniority in office.

Theoretically when a judge of the Court of Session decided a case he did so on behalf of the whole court but if a party or parties to the case were dissatisfied with his judgment, within a time fixed by rules of court, they could reclaim to the Inner House. This had the effect that the Inner House reviewed the judgment of the judge sitting in the Outer House and if necessary altered his decision so that the new decision became the decision of the Lords of Counsel and Session. If a matter arising in the case had already been decided by a division in a way that appeared to the judges taking part to have been doubtful, a larger court of five or seven or even consisting of the whole court could be convened. The doctrine of binding precedent has never been so firmly established in Scotland as it has south of the border and it was always accepted that opinions of courts of larger numbers of judges could overrule decisions made by fewer. A similar development was proposed in England by Lord Denning when he was Master of the Rolls, but as not infrequently happened, his initiative was not taken up by the House of Lords.

The Court of Session also has appellate jurisdiction from the Sheriff Court as well as from a large number of tribunals. These normally go directly to the Inner House and are taken by one or other of the divisions. The judges who constitute the Court of Session are the same as those who constitute the High Court of Justiciary. The Lord President of the Court of Session when presiding in the High Court changes his title to be Lord Justice General.

The High Court hears appeals by case stated from the district court and the sheriff court in summary criminal matters. By statute there has now been constituted a Scottish Court of Criminal Appeal of which the judges are also the judges of the Court of Session and the High Court of Justiciary. The Court of Criminal Appeal hears appeals in solemn cases against sentence and conviction. Appeal to the House of Lords lies only in civil cases. The history of how this came to happen is extremely interesting but I think it would not be appropriate for me to dwell on it now.

The court structure in Northern Ireland is broadly similar to that in England and Wales, although of course the courts are much smaller.

I think that the very distinctive feature of the court system in England and Wales which makes it so different from all other systems that I have come to know, is the emphasis placed on the lay magistracy. It is a very special tribute to the voluntary spirit and its strength in England and Wales that some 29,000 citizens are prepared to give substantially of their time and energy to the work of the lay magistracy, without financial reward of any sort and very limited reimbursement of expenses. Although similar systems were put into operation in other countries following the English pattern, I do not know of any in which it has survived with anything like the strength that obtains in England and Wales. This justice administered locally, by local people broadly representative of the community, is I think much to be prized. I do not believe that it is easy to replicate this system anywhere else.

The feature of the Scottish system which I particularly value is a court of very general jurisdiction, the Sheriff Court. Again this is a locally based court, although the units within which it is operated are quite large - six in all - embracing the whole of Scotland. I believe that this pattern of local courts with wide general jurisdiction in which the judges are lawyers of broad experience, has much to commend it. It is convenient for citizens to have their disputes resolved as near to their homes or places of work as possible. Obviously competitions for convenience can arise between parties at opposite ends of the country, but speaking generally I believe that a court of this type has much to commend it. The recent changes in the jurisdiction of the County Court in England and Wales has brought it much more into line with the civil part of the Sheriff Court than hitherto, and I personally believe that this is a good development and may well profitably be taken further. This development was initiated by the judges of the High Court, particularly in the Queen's Bench Division, and was then followed up by the statutory provisions which now operate.

In England and Wales, the Criminal Court with professional judges is organised differently as a result of Lord Beeching's consideration of the matter. The Crown Court embraces two distinct levels of judge as I mentioned earlier - the circuit judges and the High Court judges - with arrangements for allocation between them which are defined by practice directions given by the Lord Chief Justice in agreement with the Lord Chancellor. At one stage in the Civil Justice Review[1], a proposal was considered for the civil court to be organised on the same basis. The Civil Justice Review eventually recommended continuing with the two distinct levels of court, the County Court and the High Court, but suggested that steps should be taken to align their procedures more closely so as to facilitate transfer between the courts. For my part, I consider that a distinct court with a comparatively small number of judges at the higher level is a very beneficial type of structure. I personally am extremely glad this this was the arrangement which ultimately the Civil Justice Review came to favour. I do believe that there is great merit in there being at the top of the judicial hierarchy a group of judges recognised in the profession as of the highest quality in a distinct court, appointment to which marks them out to the general public.

But this arrangement does immediately pose the question of the extent to which the services of such a court should be locally available. It has been customary in Scotland for the Court of Session to sit only in Edinburgh. Although that has given rise to debate from time to time the position seems generally to be accepted. In England and Wales on the

---

[1] The Report of the Review Body on Civil Justice was published in June 1988 (Cm. 394).

other hand it has been customary, particularly for Queen's Bench work, for this to be dealt with by High Court judges on circuit. This has also been true more recently of Family Division work. I believe that this has been a useful feature of the High Court in this country and, for myself, I would like to see it extended. In the Chancery Division the Vice-Chancellor of the County Palatine does go to the north of England and I believe that this is very acceptable there and has helped to stimulate lawyers in the North to provide specialist Chancery services to their clients. I believe that this is healthy for the profession as well as beneficial to the clients since they are able to have their disputes heard by senior judges near to their homes or place of business.

In the long term, I would hope to see further developments on these lines, for example in relation to the work of the High Court in judicial review, where it might often be convenient for cases to be heard at centres such as Birmingham, Liverpool, Newcastle, Leeds, Bristol or Cardiff. On the other hand, my personal belief is that the quality and unity of the High Court is served by its base being in the Royal Courts of Justice in the Strand. Here the judges are in close contact with one another and have an opportunity of sitting with their colleagues in the Court of Appeal (Criminal Division) as well as in the Divisional Court.

Since its inception, the Court of Appeal has always sat in London, although the Court of Appeal (Criminal Division) has experimented with sitting outside London. My understanding is that these experiments were not thought to have been very successful and I think that there is merit in having work of this character centralised in London. As I have said earlier, the more courtrooms that one can assemble and use together the more flexibly one can deal with the workload and the better one can accommodate the convenience of parties and their advisors. I would regard it as unlikely that the purposes of justice would be better served by the Courts of Appeal moving, except to a very limited degree and probably only in exceptional circumstances.

The actual trial or making the decision in a case is not the only part of the administration of justice. The judge presides in a court so a court building has to be provided. The judge requires staff, an associate or clerk and an usher. The judge can hear only one case at a time and he will be powerless to proceed, however anxious he may be to make progress, if a person essential to that progress is absent. The proceedings require the presence of parties with their legal representatives, if they are so represented. In actions involving questions of disputed fact the presence of witnesses may be required and in cases which are decided by juries, arrangements must be made for the presence of a sufficient number of jurors to enable the case to proceed. The bringing of a potential juror to court is a matter of sending out the necessary document in good time and with suitable information. This necessarily must be done some time in advance of the date fixed for the trial. The parties and their witnesses must be informed and, so far as possible, their convenience taken into account. Once the case has begun and proceeds from one day to the next the arrangements have to be made for the attendance of all those who have a necessary part in the proceedings.

The assignment of a date for a case to proceed is usually known as "listing" in England and Wales. It would, I think, be regarded as a waste of the judges' time for them to have to make the detailed arrangements attempting to suit parties' convenience. The discussions for these are sometimes prolonged, sometimes acrimonious, and often subject to repeated adjustment. It is obviously right that an officer with administrative experience should be responsible, subject to judicial supervision, for this process. Where a case is disposed of substantially on paperwork, the amount of administration required to enable the case to proceed is a great deal less than when it involves a substantial oral hearing or trial. When the difficulties of arranging oral hearings are emphasised, it is wise to take account of the fact that the alternative method involves a great restriction on witnesses confronting one another or the parties, which is an important feature of the judicial process on disputed facts in this country.

This process of listing is one which is subject to a good deal of criticism. I have seen suggestions that listing should be an administrative process. By this I think is meant that the judges should have no part in it, that it should be arranged purely by administrators. As I have said, it is obvious that the detailed arrangements should be in the hands of an administrator, but I consider that it must be appropriate for a party or a witness to have ultimate recourse to the judge to decide whether or not a case should go ahead on a particular day, whether a particular witness needs to attend on a particular day. This I think demonstrates that the ultimate control of the listing process has to be in the hands of the judge, and the attitude which the judge takes to listing will have an important effect on the way in which cases are disposed of in his court. For example, early in my tenure of office as Lord Chancellor I went to a County Court in the centre of London in which the backlog was small although the court was busy. I quickly learned that the reason for this was that once a case was in the list for a particular date only the strongest possible reason would allow it to be removed. The consequence was that lawyers involved in that court knew that they had to prepare the case in time to enable it to proceed and that if they wished to consider negotiations for settlement they should conduct them in good time before the date fixed. Of course, where a good reason emerges justice may require a case to be dropped from the list.

Many considerations play a part in the listing of cases and I believe that it is important that the judge who has responsibility for the court in question should be involved in settling the policy to be pursued by the listing officer. This is an area of the administration of justice in our country which is, as I have said, often the subject of criticism particularly from professionals and those who may be involved in particular cases. The professional often emphasises the right of the client to choose his advocate. It is obvious that if this were to be extended too far and a particular advocate became well known and popular - and undoubtedly there are some well known names in this connection - the courts might find that they could only have two or three courts operating at a time because all these advocates were engaged in them and the remaining clients wished to have the services of one or other of these to represent them in their cases. I do not believe that the administration of justice could take place satisfactorily if this doctrine were to have too strong a place. On the other hand, the conve-

nience of those who are witnesses in the case, particularly
lay witnesses making a one-off appearance as witnesses,
requires, in my view, very careful consideration. In criminal
cases being a witness may be a very difficult experience. It is
essential that information about their convenience be available to the listing officer. We must, if our system of
administration of justice is to be acceptable, ensure that
those who perform their public duty as witnesses in proceedings before the court have their convenience taken into
account in relation to their giving evidence.

However there is also a duty to turn up at the appropriate
time when called. I have had repeated accounts of cases in
which witnesses have turned up at the court time after time
only to find that someone else vital to the case was not there
and therefore the case had to be postponed. I bear in mind
that one of the functions of these lectures is to emphasise
the responsibilities attaching to our system. I believe that in
many cases the continental systems require considerably less
oral evidence and therefore less personal attendance than
do ours. If the value of our more oral system is to be
retained, as I certainly think it should, the importance of
those being required to attend court doing so faithfully in
accordance with their responsibilities is vital. Their failure
can cause great inconvenience to others.

But the administration does not end there. The case in
question is not the only case which the court has to
consider. There are further cases waiting. In order to fix
these it is necessary to have some idea of how long the case
before the court is likely to take so that arrangements can
be made for the following case to be brought on. The
prediction of how long a particular case is likely to take
represents an important part of the listing process and I
believe it is one in which all engaged bear a considerable
responsibility. Arrangements made to bring a case on
sometimes fail. They can fail completely as when, for
example, a vital witness does not show and the case cannot
proceed without that witness. But the trial can also fail
because at the last minute either the prosecution states that
it will call no evidence, or the accused decides to plead
guilty to a charge or charges either as originally indicted or
as amended and accepted by the prosecution.

The so-called "cracked trial" is an important and difficult phenomenon. Obviously once the accused has accepted his guilt or the Crown has decided not to proceed, there is no question of requiring a trial. On the other hand, jurors and witnesses will have been brought to court on the understanding that the trial was to proceed. If these matters had been resolved just a few days earlier, but preferably a few weeks earlier, the inconvenience to a great number of people could have been avoided. It is often said that an accused person does not want to decide, and particularly to take a decision with adverse consequences, until he is absolutely required to do so. This may be a factor in many cases but there are also cases in which the Crown decides to present no evidence. The position must be capable of resolution earlier than the morning of the trial. Various efforts have been made to improve matters in this area. The Royal Commission on Criminal Justice[2] has made a considerable number of recommendations designed to do just this.

It is sometimes said that listing is done for the convenience of the judges and on the basis that a judge must not be kept waiting. I do not agree at all with the suggestion that judicial supervision and responsibility for listing leads to the judges taking the view that their convenience is the most important factor to be taken into account. It is vitally important that the resources provided in the judicial system are reasonably used. If a court is not used for any substantial period of time and there is a waiting list of cases to be tried, then there is obviously a delay which it could, it might appear, be avoided in the hearing of that case. Now obviously it is impossible, for practical considerations such as I have mentioned, to fill every court, every day, even where there is a prolonged waiting list. But the desire to press on with the list and to try to get as many cases disposed of as justly and efficiently as can be accommodated is surely a very proper consideration. I therefore strongly support the view that the judicial policy on listing properly takes account of this factor. Arrangements for a particular trial involve a considerable amount of administration. I

[2] Report of the Royal Commission on Criminal Justice, July 1993 (Cm. 2263).

believe that it is right that that administration is the responsibility of the appropriate judge of the court in question and that listing is a judicial function in that sense.

As I said earlier, there are much wider matters than the listing of particular cases in a particular court which fall into the category of administration. The provision of court buildings, the provision of staff, the arrangements for their remuneration and arrangements for support services all come to mind. The related agencies have to be considered, for example, in the field of criminal justice, the police, the Crown Prosecution Service, prisons, the probation service, the social services, and others.

To carry out this administration so far as the courts that are organised on a national basis is concerned, is the function of the Court Service provided by the Lord Chancellor. The Court Service is arranged with a headquarters in the Lord Chancellor's Department and six Circuits, corresponding to the circuits in the Bar of England and Wales, each under the responsibility of a Circuit Administrator. The Head of the Court Service convenes the Circuit Administrators regularly as the Court Service Board and representatives of the Scottish Courts Administration and the Northern Ireland Court Service attend, as does the Official Solicitor. The courts in the Circuits are grouped under the Circuit Administrators, with Courts Administrators responsible for each of the groups and the individual courts being administered by Chief Clerks. The administration of the Court Service is paralleled in the judicial structure by the Senior Presiding Judge and the Presiding Judges for each Circuit. These are responsible to the Lord Chief Justice, as President of the Queen's Bench Division and of the Criminal Division of the Court of Appeal, and to the Lord Chancellor, as President of the Supreme Court, which includes the Crown Court, for directing the judicial arrangements in the circuits. There are senior Circuit Judges with responsibility for directing judicial arrangements in larger court centres, for example the Recorder of Liverpool and the Recorder of London. In smaller centres, resident judges have corresponding responsibilities.

I intend to improve the administration of the courts of England and Wales by creating an Executive Agency to give the administrative support to the judges which it is the responsibility of the Lord Chancellor to provide. This agency will have the characteristics of other agencies which have been successfully established in the last few years, for example the Land Registry and the Public Record Office in the Lord Chancellor's area of responsibility. It will have a Chief Executive, responsible to the Lord Chancellor, but with a degree of freedom of operation within a framework set down at its inception. The Agency will be expected to work to deliver the service which the administration of justice requires. One of the key features of a successful Agency will be the arrangements for co-operation with the judges.

In my opinion, the successful administration of justice depends on close co-operation between the judiciary and the members of the Court Service at the headquarters level, at the circuit level and at the level of the court centres. It will be necessary in the framework document of the new Agency to articulate these arrangements, but the primary necessity is a mutual understanding between the judges and their supporting officials, with a unity of purpose in what they seek to achieve. As I have said, it would be a misuse of the judges' time to immerse them in the minutiae of administration. On the other hand, it is crucial in my view that the administrators who support the judges understand the judicial policy and seek to carry it out in detail in the areas affected.

The difficulty of setting up the Court Service as an Agency is perhaps highlighted by the difficulty of setting meaningful targets for that Service. Publishing such targets will be a key element in delivering improved levels of service to court users. This is not so difficult where the Service is providing routine administration such as the issue of process, the issuing of orders, the execution and return on warrants, handling of correspondence, making facilities for witnesses and jurors available, and dealing with the summoning of jurors, their accommodation and maintaining communication with them. It would be possible readily to set targets because most of these matters would be within the control of the administration itself.

Matters become somewhat more difficult when we move out of these areas of the Court Service's work into areas which are more directly connected with the judicial work of the courts. There are many players in the justice system, all of whom can have an impact on the effectiveness or otherwise of the courts. In these circumstances there can be difficulties for the administration in considering the average length of time between committal and start of a trial in the Crown Court, or from committal to the completion of a trial. Before a trial can start the parties to it must be prepared and on the day in question their witnesses must be present and so on. The length of time taken after a committal by the prosecution to prepare its case, or the availability of the defendant's counsel is not a matter within the control of the administration. Using notional dates such as the date on which the court could provide a courtroom and an appropriate judge can be imperfect, if the trial did not start at that time for other reasons. To use the time to the end of the trial as the measure obviously involves matters such as the succinctness or otherwise of the advocacy, the degree of control by the judge, the loquacity or otherwise of witnesses, the length of time for which the jury deliberated, and so on. The move to Agency status will require careful examination of these difficult issues.

Problems superficially similar to this arise in other areas. For example in relation to the work of Health Authorities. But in my view these are greater in the case of the Court Service since the most important participants in the court's work are the judges, who do not belong to the executive arm of Government. These are difficulties yet to be faced in connection with the decision to set up the Court Service as an Agency. However I do believe that we must try to develop techniques for assessing the efficiency of the Court Service in its administrative work and that it will be quite a spur to this search that I have set a date by which I hope the Court Service will be established as an Agency.[3] When this happens it will, I think, contribute of itself to the efficiency of the administration of the courts, particularly in those areas which are not so close to the date to day work of the judges as are the conduct of trials and hearings.

The Court Service currently comprises some 90 centres dealing with criminal business and 290 dealing with civil

[3] April 1995.

business; at 39 of these locations the work is handled in Combined Court Centres. Together, they occupy a total of 407 buildings, and are supported by the use of 139 buildings hired for occasional use. The Supreme Court and Principal Registry of the Family Division occupy 5 buildings in London including the Royal Courts of Justice and Somerset House, and are supported by a network of 11 District Registries, 18 Probate Sub-Registries, and 91 Probate Offices.

Of the centres with County Court jurisdiction, 82 are trial centres, 51 are jointly Care and Family Hearing centres, whilst a further 51 are designated only as Family Hearing Centres. There remain a small number of "caller offices" which are manned part-time. Since its inception in 1971 the court building programme has seen the introduction of 129 schemes. Of these, 27 have been Combined Court Centres, 62 Crown Courts and 32 County Courts. In addition there have been 5 schemes for the High Court and 3 miscellaneous schemes. The programme has, so far, provided a total of 366 new criminal courtrooms (a net increase of 209), 76 civil courtrooms (an increase of 20), 10 dual purpose courtrooms (an increase of 6) and 27 High Court courtrooms (an increase of 17). There are currently 12 schemes under construction with 9 in design and 11 in the pre-planning stage. Together these will add a further 154 criminal courtrooms, 43 civil courtrooms, 4 dual purpose courtrooms, and 16 High Court courtrooms. Half of the proposed new buildings will be Combined Court centres.

The remaining courts and offices are a mixture of old, purpose built courts and converted, leasehold, office accommodation. Many are now unsuitable for their current purpose with inadequate facilities or capacity, and with little scope for extension or conversion. However 110 buildings on the estate are listed as being of architectural or historic importance; in many cases this limits the scope for extension or adaptation to meet changing operational requirements.

An important consideration in relation to courts in the administration of justice is to ensure that sufficient and adequate courtrooms exist. This means addressing questions such as what number of courtrooms or ancillary accommodation will be needed over the next decade; where, when and for how long; and to what standard. The challenge for the administration is to make the most effective use of limited resources to meet those needs. For example, in civil business, changing needs and priorities are currently apparent. The programme of initiatives rooted in the Civil Justice Review and the Children Act have secured changes which have a clear accommodation dimension: the centralisation of hearings/trials; the centralisation and computerisation of debt processing; the emergence of differing accommodation requirements between the component businesses of civil business (for example, debt and family); judicial specialisation; reduction in the need for attendance; and the pushing down of cases to an appropriate level in the court structure and devolution with concurrent jurisdiction at lower level for circuit and district judges.

These influences on the desired pattern and nature of civil work have already resulted in accommodation changes, in particular, the development of a network of trial centres to deal with civil cases requiring hearings, the introduction of the Summons Production Centre (which uses the more modern technology to produce, as its name implies, a very large number of summonses, over 1,000,000 per annum) and the development of Family Hearing and Care Centres which recognise the particular accommodation characteristics of family business. The changes will not always be so specific and tangible and it is not possible to define a "template" to which the estate must be made to fit. Equally it is clear that the influences which I have just mentioned will continue to impact on the nature and shape of the court network.

The policy of encouraging combination of courts in one court centre is a recent and important development. It was introduced when the overriding need was the flexibility required to cope with a substantially increased workload. It was more, however, than an opportunistic response. Combined courts were considered to offer three important, potential benefits: first, the more flexible deployment of judicial resources; secondly, greater flexibility in the use of staff and economies of scale in the provision of common services; and, finally, and this is extremely important, greater simplicity in meeting the service needs of the public. Some of these advantages have been realised and remain very relevant. Obviously, there is continuing value in being able to direct the public to a single centre and, on the judicial front, combined courts have provided a greater flexibility which has not been inhibited by limited moves towards judicial specialisation. Combination has also delivered flexibility in the allocation and training of staff, particularly in smaller courts.

Notwithstanding this success, especially in generating a wider perception of the Lord Chancellor Department's activities, there have been some disappointments. Despite combination, few combined courts are fully integrated. The County Courts, unlike the Crown Court, cannot maintain a consistent balance between courtroom and office requirements in relation to the number of courtrooms. The need for County Court office space is changeable and the need bears no direct correlation to courtroom needs. To that extent, therefore, Combined Court Centres artificially restrict the accommodation options for County Courts.

This brings me to consider another matter which is important in relation to the administration of the courts. As I explained in my first lecture, the Lord Chancellor is charged with providing the administrative staff for the work of the courts, and the budget of the courts is part of the budget which Parliament has assigned to the Lord Chancellor. Because of his dual capacity he can be made accountable to Parliament for the whole work of the courts, although in doing so he and Parliament must respect the principle of the independence of the judiciary, as I sought to explain it last time.

In the Federal jurisdictions in the Commonwealth of Australia, a system has been developed, starting with the High Court, in which the administration of the court is a matter for the court itself, the court being assigned a sum of money with which to perform its work. This has applied to the High Court and then separately to the Federal Court and has now also been applied again separately to the Family Court. It is early days in this process and I shall certainly watch with interest how it develops. The smaller and more compact the court is, and the High Court of

Australia has a comparatively small complement, the easier it is to prepare a budget and to adhere to it. The more diverse and larger the structure is the more difficult it is to accomplish this task and I shall be particularly interested to see how this process is adapted to the work of the Family Court. From the point of view of the Government there are attractions in fixing a budget for a court and leaving the court to get on with its administration. For this purpose it would be necessary I think for the head of the court to have the primary responsibility, but being a judge on secure tenure, and security of tenure is generally necessary as underpinning the independence of the judiciary, there is no basis upon which he can be accountable to Parliament for the way in which the money is spent and the manner in which the courts are administered. Therefore, if things go wrong a difficult situation could arise. Under our system, which I think is neither strictly speaking an executive model nor a judicial model of administration, the Lord Chancellor, although the President of the Supreme Court and a member both of that court and of the House of Lords and of the Judicial Committee of the Privy Council, does so without any security of tenure and therefore when he is responsible for the administration if things go wrong it is possible to get rid of him readily and secure a replacement. Although the day to day administration is carried out under the responsibility of the Lord Chancellor, I have no doubt that the fact that the Lord Chancellor is thus responsible is an important part of the chain of accountability between the Court Service and Parliament.

The development of the Court Service as an agency will help to ensure a clear distinction between the rest of the Lord Chancellor's Departments and the Court Service. If this development succeeds, as I believe it will, new possibilities may open up for the administration of the courts but in the British situation as I see it at present and for the future so far as I can see it, I consider that any move to making the professional judiciary who are tenured responsible for the administration of the courts and for the administration of the Vote for the courts, to the House of Commons, would be an extremely retrograde and confusing step. The support of the courts in these matters are, in my view, the duty and the responsibility of the executive and should be clearly seen to remain so.

In the next lecture I shall consider the role of the legal profession in the administration of justice with particular emphasis in their work in the courts.

3. Legal Services

This evening I wish to talk about legal services. I shall concentrate in my remarks on those services in relation to the administration of justice. Therefore, I shall not make reference to legal services in uncontentious business nor to the notaries and other professional bodies more or less closely related to solicitors and barristers. Traditionally in England and Wales legal services to the public have been provided by the two branches of the legal profession, solicitors and barristers, both consisting of individuals in private practice - solicitors practising either alone or in partnership with other solicitors; barristers always practising alone and not in partnership with other barristers, albeit arranged in chambers with chambers' administration and a staff of clerks with permissible arrangements for sharing of costs. Similar arrangements prevail in Northern Ireland although there barristers practice from the library with administration for the whole Bar and therefore with a minimum of overhead costs.

In Scotland the equivalent of a barrister is a member of the Faculty of Advocates. Just to confuse matters there are also advocates in Aberdeen but they are not members of the Faculty of Advocates but members of the Law Society and therefore equivalent to solicitors. In former times members of the Faculty of Advocates generally lived in the New Town of Edinburgh and practised from their homes. They normally came up to court in time for the start of the "day" at about 9.30 and went down after the court rose. They had their consultations with solicitors and clients in their homes in the late afternoon or early evening. Papers were delivered from Parliament House to the home of each advocate about 6.00 or 7.00 o'clock in the evening and

papers were returned from the advocates' homes to the
Parliament House at an unearthly hour in the morning, so
that they were there for the advocate when he arrived.
During the day, if not engaged in court, advocates worked
in the advocates' library and were available for consultation
with solicitors or instruction by them, if necessary at short
notice, in the library. Each member of faculty in practice
had a clerk and the clerk served a fairly large number of
advocates, although the services he provided were generally
less than those provided to members of the Bar in England
by the clerks in their Chambers. The fact that the advocates
practised from Parliament House to the extent that I have
described helped to minimise their overheads and also gave
members of Faculty in practice a cohesion which was useful
in keeping up to date with changes in practice and many of
the advantages of being in chambers in England were in this
way available, although the practicability of these arrangements depended upon the Bar being relatively small.

In recent times many advocates have chosen to live
outside the area convenient for the arrangements I have
described. More and more members of the Faculty of
Advocates work within Parliament House and use the
advocates' library as their place for consultation after court
as well as during the day. The weight of criminal work done
outside Edinburgh in the High Court, particularly in
Glasgow, has meant that it is now practicable for members
of the Scots Bar who work predominantly in the High
Court, particularly in Glasgow, to live in the West of
Scotland.

Another noteworthy feature of the Scottish system is that
advocates' papers were set out in boxes, each with the
advocate's name on the front, in the court corridors in
Parliament House. This was indeed an extremely open
system but I am not aware of it ever having been abused. It
is an interesting fact that arrangements of this kind develop
very much to suit the circumstances of the profession they
serve. The English Bar tried an experiment to provide
library facilities in the Inns of Court for members of the Bar
who could not obtain tenancies, but it did not succeed. The
Scottish and Northern Irish methods of working were
carefully studied before the English experiment was set up,

but it was never intended to replace the current system in England of barristers chambers and its principal difficulty was that those in the library had to compete with those in more ready contact with solicitors through being tenants in chambers.

I now turn to look more particularly at the arrangements for providing legal services in England and Wales and very generally the principles of these arrangements apply also in Scotland and Northern Ireland.

In order to obtain a legal service, a member of the public would have recourse to a solicitor or solicitor's firm. In former times lawyers were prohibited by their own rules from advertising and so a member of the public seeking a service had to rely on reputation, or recommendation, or perhaps a fortuitous meeting on the basis of which the selection of a solicitor would be made. Where a client who had a solicitor required the services of a barrister, it was the solicitor's responsibility to make the choice of the appropriate barrister. The solicitor's knowledge of the Bar was relied upon to enable him to make a wise and suitable choice for the particular case in hand. The two branches of the profession are self-regulating, although the solicitors' branch does so under a fairly elaborate framework of statutory provisions while the Bar is regulated by the Inns of Court with very little in the way of statutory framework. In recent times the Bar has been divided into two levels, the junior Bar and the Queen's Counsel or senior Bar. No such distinction has obtained between members of the solicitors' branch, although as I shall mention later, there is at present the possibility of solicitors receiving honorary silk and in due course, if solicitors obtain rights of audience in the Higher Courts[1], they will become eligible for practising silk as well. In more recent times the Institute of Legal Executives has given formal recognition to the status of persons practising law without the full qualification required to become a solicitor but often with immense practical experience of work done by solicitors.

[1] It was announced on December 8, 1993 that solicitors in private practice would be eligible to appear in the Higher Courts.

The lawyers to whom I have referred as serving the public are remunerated by means of fees paid by their clients. Generally speaking these fees are unregulated and therefore a lawyer is entitled to make any arrangement he wishes about the amount he will charge his client, though this may be subject to scrutiny by the courts. Since the fees payable for services given in connection with litigation are substantial, the cost of these services form a most important consideration in the administration of justice. It is perfectly possible for a member of the public who wishes to resort to the courts to do so without the assistance of a lawyer, as a litigant in person. Because of the complexities of the substantive law as well as of the legal process, substantial hurdles stand in the way of a litigant in person and the successful pursuit of an action. But in general, since this route is available, anyone has access to justice, although the burden that may be placed on the court in doing justice may be much greater than it would if the litigant were adequately represented by lawyers.

In our system, as I have said, the client first chooses his or her solicitor. A new leaflet from the National Consumer council "Getting the best from your Solicitor" should assist in this process and is to be welcomed. At this early stage the client may be given, and I believe should be given, a clear statement of the basis on which the solicitor will charge for the legal services to be provided. This should include of course the outlays that may be necessary for securing the help of expert witnesses or representation by counsel if the litigation is to be in a court where the solicitor does not have rights of audience, or where after consultation with his lay client, the solicitor decides to instruct counsel. Even where the basis of charging is made clear and precise, it will be extremely difficult to furnish the client in most contested litigation with any reliable estimate of the total amount which he may ultimately require to pay for legal services under the current arrangements. This may be difficult for the client to grasp but I regard it as of great importance that the risks of litigation and the unpredictability of the outcome should be clearly set out at an early stage. The Law Society Practice Management standards encourage solicitors to do this.

It is vital that the solicitor explains how the various unpredictable elements of litigation may affect the pattern of costs. The initial stages of the litigation may be capable of reasonably precise estimations of their cost, but once a litigation is embarked upon, it cannot be stopped at the instance of the plaintiff without at least the risk of cost because of the general rule obtaining in this country that the court has power to make an award against one party of the costs incurred by another. It is crucial that this should be explained clearly by solicitors to their clients. Indeed, as I shall come to mention later, Parliament has conferred a very wide discretion on the court in this connection. But the matter becomes even more dramatic once the preliminary stages are passed because when a trial is embarked upon it is extremely difficult to say how long it may last, and the system of payments for legal services is quite heavily dependent on the length of the trial. Even after trial, there is of course the question of appeal and even of a second appeal. At every stage there are options of withdrawal and possible settlement, which should be explained to clients as the case proceeds, but again there is always a risk of an adverse award of costs incurred by another party to the litigation. Against this background, and the difficulty of estimating what a person may be risking in embarking on litigation, it is no wonder that the costs of obtaining the necessary legal services are regarded as an important impediment to obtaining justice.

So far, lawyers have generally charged for cases in such a way as to pass the risk of the length of time for which the case will last on to the client, on a basis similar to the cost plus basis in ordinary contracting. Hitherto, it was not lawful in England and Wales for a lawyer to arrange with the lay client that the lay client would have to pay the lawyer's fee if and only if the litigation was successful. The Courts and Legal Services Act has now made such an arrangement lawful. I am in the course of preparing the necessary subordinate legislation to bring a provision into effect to allow that the lay client be required to pay his lawyers if and only if the case succeeds. The precise definition of success will be a matter of some importance to be settled between them. Since the risk of the litigation's failure is an important factor, I have accepted the view expressed by the Law Society on consultation that the uplift to be permitted should be a maximum of 100 per cent. In other words, if the case succeeds the client may have to pay up to twice the fee which ordinarily would be payable if the client were paying on the ordinary basis. This 100 per cent is, of course, intended as the maximum uplift that will be allowed by law. There is nothing to prevent a solicitor agreeing to be paid, if the litigation is successful, a sum less than this maximum and indeed agreeing to be paid a fixed sum determined in advance so long as it is under the ceiling as it applies in the particular case.

I believe that the shape of litigation in this country might well be profoundly affected if lawyers took on litigation on the basis of a stated fee, determined in advance. It might well be that this would only cover a certain stage in the litigation, for example up to judgment at first instance. There is a growing tendency amongst commercial concerns seeking advice and assistance in commercial transactions to bargain for a fixed fee and to seek competitive tenders from firms able to give the service required. The more general the tendency to require a fixed fee to be negotiated in advance, the more profound would become the effect.

As I have remarked, it is one of the characteristic features of our system that the court has power to award the costs incurred by others in the litigation against a party to it. The decision of the House of Lords in *Interbulk*[2] emphasises the very wide discretion which Parliament conferred upon the courts to award costs. And the particular circumstances of interlocking arbitrations which gave rise to that case is a good illustration of how the courts by construction can impose artificial limits on a wide discretion granted by Parliament which particular events may show to have been ill-advised. Although, as I have said, the discretion is very wide, the ordinary rule is that costs follow success and therefore that the successful litigant recovers the costs incurred in the litigation against the losing party or parties. In the United States of America on the other hand, the general rule - although there are now some legislated innovations on it - is that each party bears his or her own costs.

[2] *Aiden Shipping Co. Ltd. v. Interbulk* [1986 2 Lloyd's Reports 117].

It is easy to see that a powerful economic unit can use this process to exhaust completely the funds of a party who is weaker economically. That party is then paralysed from pursuing litigation to what might in justice be a successful outcome. I believe that our costs rule is an important safeguard against conduct of this sort as well as being an important safeguard against unjustified litigation.

Should there be limits to this principle? Well, there have been limitations imposed under the Legal Aid Act in respect of awards of costs against a legally aided party.[3] This means that when legal aid is granted the party receives a double benefit. Not only is his own cost defrayed by the taxpayer, but his opponent is seriously limited in the costs that he may be awarded against the legally aided client. Thus a party who obtains legal aid has the very important benefit that he knows exactly where he stands. He can be told at what rate he will have to contribute, although the precise amount he must pay will be determined by the length of the case; and he can receive very firm advice about the amount that is likely to be the maximum awarded against him if he loses. If he succeeds most of his contributions are likely to be refunded. If his opponent is a person just over the legal aid limit one can see the scope for considerable injustice, although that injustice is mitigated to some extent if the provisions of severe hardship can be satisfied. It has been argued strongly, for example by Lord Simon of Glaisdale, that it is unjust that the non-legally aided party, if successful in the litigation, should not be able to recover his costs and in the circumstances this could only be from the taxpayer.[4]

The strength of this argument must be recognised, but the priorities in relation to preventing injustice have to be weighed. Hitherto Parliament has approved an arrangement under which the taxpayer's money is used primarily to assist those of poor or moderate means who have a reasonable case to litigate rather than to limit the amount of assistance

[3] Section 18 of the Legal Aid Act 1988.

[4] Official Reports, January 18, 1988, col. 57-58, February 4, 1988, col. 1255-56, 1259-1260.

given in this way, and spend the balance of the money available from the taxpayer in defraying the costs of litigants successful against legally aided parties. The main problem, so far as legal aid is concerned, is the need to limit the provision that the taxpayer makes for this service. In criminal matters it has been found quite hard to do so. Comparatively few of those who seek criminal legal aid are in a position to make a contribution. Where they are in such a position, they sometimes elect not to do so and refuse legal aid with consequences to themselves and to the possibility of a fair trial.

This brings me to consider the question of litigants in person. Where an individual is entitled to plead his own or her own case without legal representation, a particular stress is put upon the judge. This was adverted to in the letter which my colleagues the Lord Chief Justice and the Master of the Rolls wrote to me in connection with revision of legal aid eligibility last year.[5] The letter referred particularly to the situation in the Court of Appeal. Not very long before, the previous Master of the Rolls had raised the question of legal aid being made available in the Court of Appeal in respect of cases which seemed unworthy.[6] Apart from the waste of public money involved in providing legal aid, this also unnecessarily took up the time of the court so that there is obviously a balance to be struck between these two approaches. Where people are refused legal aid or do not wish to have it, do not wish to employ lawyers at their own expense and cannot obtain free assistance, they will be obliged, if they wish to pursue the case, to do it themselves. Part of the motivation for the small claims court and its informal system is to enable people with no particular expertise in the law to pursue their claims. I believe that on the whole this system is reasonably effective for this purpose and we have endeavoured to provide forms and help which will make the procedure as comprehensible as

[5] The letter was also referred to in the *Official Report*, House of Lords, February 3, 1993, col. 283.

[6] Official Report, House of Lords, November 17, 1992, col. 590.

possible and as easy to use as it can be for those inexperienced in the law.

There are, however, limits to what can be done. The basic substance of law is complicated, even in relation to quite simple transactions. However in many cases I believe the important questions are questions of fact and the capacity for explaining in reasonable order how the problem has arisen is the primary quality required of a litigant in person. Judges are expected to know the law and the emphasis on judicial training in recent years has assisted in making that expectation a reality. I would suggest that to have a system of reasonably straightforward procedure, such as we have in the small claims court, is highly desirable in the interests of full access to justice for ordinary people; and that in very many cases where issues of fact are involved it is satisfactory. I do not believe that a system is really just when it requires a person seeking to recover a particular sum to expend for that purpose an amount which is a very high proportion of that sum. The Civil Justice Review showed than in far too many cases, for example of personal injury, the cost of pursuing a claim was a very high proportion of the money recovered.

It is natural, therefore, as I have done, to seek to extend the small claims system to this type of case. There are, however, difficulties about doing so. One of the attractive features of the small claims system is that no costs are required to be incurred for lawyers' services and only very small amounts of money are therefore at risk by way of costs. The fear of attracting costs is removed as an inhibition in this type of case. But if a person seeks to recover damages for personal injury he will normally need to obtain a medical report detailing his injuries and possibly the evidence of an expert or at least evidence from someone with special experience in the practice involved in the circumstances of the accident - for example, the usual practice of a particular class of employer in making arrangements for the carrying out of the type of work in which the person claiming was injured. Under present circumstances these reports and advice are obtained by a lawyer and the employer, more likely his insurer, if the claim is settled before going to court, will allow as part of the settlement a reasonable sum to cover these costs as well as the cost of employing the lawyer. If one applies the small claims system to this area that approach would be considerably eroded.

It is, therefore, for consideration whether one should apply the system with modifications. A certain amount of cost could be payable by or on behalf of the employer covering such reports and advice. If the injured person succeeds he would get these costs. Would it be fair that if he loses he would not have to pay for the costs incurred by his employer obtaining like help? The employer might not need expert advice but more than likely he would need some medical report. No doubt this could be resolved to some extent by requiring that the claimant produce his medical report and the employer thus be relieved of having one for himself, unless he had some reason to challenge it, which he might do at his own expense. There is a tendency in some quarters to overlook the need to preserve a balance between the claimant and the employer - not all employers are large and wealthy concerns. The householder of modest means might be the employer and the system should be fair to them also. While perfect fairness may be impossible to attain, I believe that reasonable access to justice for many claims of this sort could be provided under a modification of the small claims system.

But how far should this go? A person who might have quite a substantial claim might well be willing to pursue it using these procedures. The higher the value of the claim, of course, the more just it would be to allow cost to accrue on either side. But the mere fact that you have a large claim does not necessarily mean you have large resources. Should the client with large resources who is defending a claim for a substantial amount against a person with small resources be bound to use a system which modifies the full rights that the wealthier person would have under the present system of litigation and its rules? Lord Woolf in his recent lecture has advocated a fast track.[7] The use of the small claims procedure will provide a model for this fast track, but how

[7] The George Bean Memorial Lecture by the Right Honourable the Lord Woolf, October 24, 1993, "The Rule of Law - is it Collapsing?"

far should it extend and at whose option should it be available? Should it omit matters that are thought necessary for justice? And if there are matters in the ordinary system which are not necessary for justice, is the correct approach not to remove these requirements from our present system, thus bringing the whole system nearer to the fast track?

I believe that we may need to approach this from two opposite standpoints. First, we should consider extending the small claims system further, with some modifications, to new classes of subject matter, such as personal injuries, and with a limit of value which could gradually be increased with experience of its operation. At the same time we should consider the process of ordinary litigation in order to simplify its procedures. For example, at present we have in the High Court a considerable number of different ways in which a process can be initiated - by originating summons, by originating motion, by writ or by petition. There is provided in the High Court Queen's Bench Division a service for solicitors and others who may resort to the office for advice from a Master on practice. It is surely remarkable that those who are qualified to undertake the conduct of business in the High Court and who receive quite considerable fees for that work from clients should require advice on matters of practice in the High Court. Now I am the first to acknowledge that the circumstances which may arise in cases proceeding in our civil courts can be extremely varied. And at present different rules are required according to the circumstances. I do not for one moment envisage that it would be possible to produce a very simple set of procedural rules which would suit all types of case. But I do firmly believe that it should be possible to produce a simpler and shorter set of rules than we presently have. I readily admit that I personally have had, as Lord Chancellor, the responsibility for adding complexity to these rules because so often and with a degree of pressure for haste particular problems have been dealt with by amendments to the rules rather than by a comprehensive reconsideration of the rules as a whole. I suspect that this development has not been confined to my term of office as Lord Chancellor but that the present state of our rules indicates clearly that this has been operating for some time. Need it continue? Is it not time to start afresh?

I think it is time to have a thorough look at the position, although it would be a pity to start afresh because we must make use of the experience we have gained. On the other hand, I do think that, for example, the Commercial Court has shown a good way forward in this matter and that even in relation to great diversity of cases and a considerable diversity of subject matters, such as are experienced in the day to day running of the Commercial Court, it is possible to produce a reasonably comprehensible and straightforward and relatively brief set of directions for procedure. The example of the Commercial Court is sufficiently strong to encourage us to make an attempt to go along this road more generally for both the High Court and the County Court and I would like to see arrangements in hand fairly soon to explore this possibility further.

One of the facts one has to take into account in planning any such operation is that any new rules themselves create a certain amount of debate about their meaning and application but I personally believe that there is sufficient scope for considerable simplification to make it worth taking this risk. The Civil Justice Review recommended that a common set of rules should be devised. They did so particularly having regard to the flexibility they wished to see between the use of the High Court and the use of the County Court. This would fit very neatly into a project such as I have described. There could be core rules that might apply throughout both courts but with special provision for particular subject matters. The criterion would be that only such additional rules should be provided as were genuinely required for the purpose of suitably dealing with that special subject matter.

One of the central areas of cost in civil litigation at the present time is related to the process of discovery. Discovery is the process by which documents held by one party relevant to the case are required to be made available for inspection by the other party. In cases of any complexity there is likely to be a substantial quantity of correspondence and other paper having some connection with the case. It may be very difficult without a close reading of very considerable amounts of paper to decide whether or not they are likely to be of use in the determination of the issues. Where a search of this character is to go on in the records of a major company, much disruption to the work can result but where the concern is a small one the need to devote effort to meeting requirements for discovery may be altogether disproportionate to the benefit. The general rules for discovery concentrating as they do on documents necessary to be produced may be perfectly justified in principle, but I do believe that if civil litigation is to be cost effective a way must be found to limit the resources that litigants require to devote to this aspect of the preparation for the trial.

A further problem arises in this connection when a claim is made that a document which otherwise would be subject to discovery would not in fact be exhibited to the other side for a reason which can be determined only by a study of the document in question. This arises particularly in relation to the public interest immunity. The basis of this doctrine is that a document should not be produced to another party if that production is likely to substantially injure the public interest. The method by which this falls to be resolved is a certificate from the appropriate Minister or other person in authority describing the nature of the document in question and giving his or her reasons why the public interest would be damaged by their production. The court has held[8] that, generally speaking, a ministerial certificate of this character would generally be given effect but that the court, following decisions of the House of Lords which first related to Scotland, has power to overrule a ministerial certificate and find that the public interest against this closure could, in the circumstances of the particular case, be outweighed by the public interest in doing justice. Where the document or documents in question are central to the case, a judge might be required to overrule the certificate. A procedure has therefore been developed for a judge to adjudicate upon this matter. It is a very special duty placed upon the judge, very clearly distinguishable from nearly all other judicial duties in that the judge is required to examine a document, the details and contents of which are not known to the other party or parties, and reach a view upon a question between

[8] *Conway v. Rimmer* [1968, 1 All E.R. 874].

them. This is a type of legal service which the judges are required to provide which is so different from the ordinary duty of doing justice between party as in my opinion to be worthy of special mention.

Similar problems are now arising sharply in the criminal courts in relation to the same matter. There is also the related question of the production of material which has been accumulated by authorities investigating crime but which they judge to be irrelevant to the case which they wish to pursue against a defendant. Until fairly recently the responsibility for producing relevant material lay with the prosecutor. Since the prosecutor will not have been himself or herself the investigator he or she will be dependent upon the investigator to put forward material relevant to the case which has been gathered in the course of the investigation. It can readily be seen that if every possible piece of information acquired in the process of a police investigation which the police judge of no value whatever in relation to the case being pursued but which might by some off-chance turn out to be relevant to the defence, is capable of being produced, the only safe way of proceeding is for all information gathered to be presented to the prosecutor for study. It is easy to see that unless some principles can be enuciated to limit this process, the system of criminal prosecution in our country is in danger of being overwhelmed by an accumulation of useless and irrelevant material. The Royal Commision[9] has considered this question and I refer to its detailed recommendations.

I have so far been considering aspects of procedure which have a consequence for the legal services to be provided and the cost thereof. I look now at another aspect of this relationship. The courts in all three law districts of the United Kingdom have been in the habit of requiring full argument in relation to disputed questions of law from the legal representatives of parties appearing before them. This is to assist the court to come to a reasoned judgment on these matters. Because of our system of precedent, these judgments will have an effect on future cases and be binding

[9] Report of the Royal Commission of Criminal Justice, July 1993, Cm. 2263.

on courts of inferior jurisdiction. This means that the cost of providing the assistance to the court in a case is at least to some extent for the benefit of the wider public who may be affected by a similar question in the future. In cases where the matter is of very general and immediate importance to a large group of prospective litigants, it may be regarded as a test case. In such a situation special considerations may affect the award of costs, but this is just a particularly striking example of a more general situation.

A further result of this general approach has been that the judges have relied upon parties, in accordance with the duties on their legal representatives, to lay out before the court all relevant authorities whether for or against the lawyer's client. Thus illuminated, the judges themselves decide the issue and give their own judgment upon it. It has been universal in our systems that the judges prepare their own judgments with such clerical and secretarial assistance as they may require. Should this continue or should the judges be supported by a staff to do their own research and investigation of the law, restricting the parties to a presentation of the facts? Where a litigant in person is involved, a particular burden may be placed on the judge and it does require consideration whether the state should provide some particular help to the judge in that situation which it does not provide where a party chooses to be represented by lawyers before the court.

With the increasing pressure in the Court of Appeal Criminal Division and now in the Civil Division of the Court of Appeal, legal staff have been provided to assist the court in analysing the issues and assisting with the arrangements for the hearing of cases. But our system remains very different from that which applies in, for example, the Supreme Court of the United States in relation to the legal services provided to our judges. In recent times, because of the increasing complexity of some trials, judges who have wished for legally qualified special assistance have been provided with help in the analysis of evidence in very complex and lengthy trials. I think it is very easy for lay people to underestimate the tremendous burden put upon a judge in presiding over such trials. This is true even in civil matters where the judge has to decide the facts himself, but

I think it is even greater where he has the responsibility at the close of the case of summing up in a balanced way and in such a way that a jury can understand issues that may have been elaborated in evidence over a long period. Appropriate support in that situation is something which I believe it is appropriate for the judge to have if he or she wishes it, although in the nature of the responsibility the judge carries, the amount of assistance and relief he can be given is necessarily rather limited. Perhaps the other side of this particular problem is that the most effective legal service that the judge, and indeed also the jury, can be given is a thorough analysis of the issues in a succinct a form as possible from both parties. How this can be achieved against the background of the onus of proof which rests on the Crown and the inherent difficulty of providing an effective sanction against a defence, which is essentially seeking to blunt the cutting edge of the prosecution's case, is one of the problems with which the Royal Commission has had to grapple. It has provided recommendations which the Government is now seeking to develop.

In seeking to confine myself to legal services associated with litigation, I have made a considerable narrowing of the total field of the provision of legal services, but the more I have thought about this subject the more difficult I think it is to say where legal services ultimately end and non-legal services begin. This is illustrated by the fact that there is no monopoly in respect of the giving of legal advice. On the other hand, there are areas which have been occupied by lawyers and in which legal qualifications are essential, although the form of these qualifications may change from time to time with the changing needs of the public we serve. But there are support services to the courts and enforcement services which are as equally important to the operation of the legal system as these. In the field of matrimonial law again the boundaries are difficult to draw and I believe that as we look to the future we must be ready to contemplate alterations in the way in which the legal system operates in order to meet the changing needs of our society. Although many of the problems which confront individuals in our society are complicated because the law by which we are regulated is itself complicated, there are many human problems which the operation of our system requires to be addressed which may need more sympathetic analysis of factual situations than a deep understanding of the complexities of the law. We need a system under which these may be addressed without engaging unnecessarily the full panoply of services which the legal system provides, but which enables those who require to rise to some specific level of advice and competence of service, to do so relatively easily. Barristers, advocates, solicitors, law centres, advice bureaux, bailiffs, mediators, arbitrators, loss adjustors, financial consultants, and many others may have a part in this. Enterprise and intiative on their part and cooperation between them may be necessary for the ordinary members of our society, to whom these lectures are addressed, to get what they require in the way of advice to pursue their rights and the understanding of their responsibilities.

4. Alternative Dispute Resolution

In my previous lectures I have looked at three aspects of the administration of justice: the judges; the courts; and legal services. All of these play their part in our system of justice. This evening I wish to bring the three together and talk about a particular area of policy. This is alternative dispute resolution. It raises issues for all three players and challenges some traditional assumptions about the way in which justice must be administered.

The general public for whom these lectures were intended might be forgiven for wondering what alternative dispute resolution means. I shall come back to this question later in my lecture, but for the moment I shall rely on Lewis Carroll.

'It seems very pretty', said Alice, 'but it's <u>rather</u> hard to understand. Somehow it seems to fill my head with ideas - only I don't exactly know what they are!'

The distinguished mathematician and master of logic who delighted young and old with the Alice stories will, I feel sure, forgive me for quoting this well-loved figure as a way of introducing my theme for this lecture.

Alternatively dispute resolution, which for the sake of brevity I shall refer to as ADR, is linked in most people's minds with alternatives to the traditional judicial process, with which it is usually favourably contrasted. 'Whatever ADR *is*' (the argument runs) 'it is quicker, cheaper, more user-friendly than the courts. It gives people an involvement in the process of resolving their disputes that is not possible in a public, formal and adversarial justice system perceived to be dominated by the abstruse procedures and recondite language of the law. It offers choice: choice of method, of procedure, of cost, of representation, of location. Because it is often quicker than judicial proceedings, it can ease burdens on the courts. Because it is cheaper, it can help to curb the upward spiral of legal costs and legal aid expenditure too, which would benefit the parties and the taxpayer.'

I have examined these propositions with considerable interest. *If* ADR possesses such beguiling superiority over most people's perception of the courts, it is a short step in logic to argue that the civil justice system should appropriate or administer the processes which give rise to that superiority, especially if by doing so we can achieve financial savings too.

In my lecture today I shall aim to expose some of the key issues which I must resolve in deciding whether the development of ADR might enhance our civil justice system. I will first outline the main factors that have influenced, and helped to focus, my consideration of this multi-faceted subject. I shall then look at what it is we *want* from our civil justice system, so that we can identify the characteristics of ADR which have the most direct bearing on these specifications. Finally, I will dwell for a while on some of the conflicting issues with which we must grapple.

Perhaps I could offer a preliminary observation which might help us to consider these issues in context. There have been many attempts throughout history to do what the proponents of ADR wish to do, namely, to balance fairness in dispute resolution with speed, informality and flexibility, and to contain costs. Not all these attempts have been successful. Commercial arbitration, and certain administrative tribunals, are two examples of mechanisms which occasionally attract criticisms of excessive legalism and delay. Indeed, the recent conference of the Chartered Institute of Arbitrators[1] had as its theme the need to escape from the rapidly encroaching "court-style procedures" which are apparently increasing cost, delay and complexity in that forum. I think there are lessons here for our present deliberations, and I shall try to draw them out in the course of my talk.

[1] Held in Glasgow on September 24, 1993.

Let me briefly mention family mediation. I do not propose to deal with this in any detail today although earlier in the week I published a consultation paper on divorce law reform and family mediation.[2] In some respects, family mediation is different from other forms of mediation and ADR. For those of you particularly interested in family mediation, I commend the consultation paper to you. You will find there the more pertinent arguments that apply in favour and against it.

Examination of ADR must take place against the background of three, or perhaps four, pertinent developments. First, it coincides with the continuing implementation of civil justice reforms. Stemming from the report of the Review Body published in 1988 and the enactment of the Courts and Legal Services Act in 1990, the aims of the reform programme share many of those often claimed for ADR. There has been emphasis on removing work from the courts which is not judicial in nature and providing the flexibility for judicial work to be done in the *right* forum and by the *right* level of judge. Procedures should be more closely tailored to the needs of particular categories of case, and court rules and procedures clarified so that they are intelligible to litigants themselves, without excessive reliance on professional advisers. The continuing commitment must be steadily to reduce the delay, cost and complexity of going to law for those who must do so and, if the development of ADR seems to offer tangible opportunities to this end, we must explore them.

A second focus for my examination of ADR has emerged from the numerous calls - from the legal and other professions, from consumer organisations, and from the business and voluntary sector - for a system of *court-annexed* mediation or arbitration. Indeed, a remarkable consensus seems to exist - with only a few whispers to the contrary - on the desirability of adopting this particular approach to bringing ADR into the court system. It therefore demands and deserves the closest attention. But not exclusively: because it is important that opportunities presented by other approaches are not neglected.

[2] *Looking to the future: mediation and the ground for divorce* December 1993; Cm. 2424.

A third factor which has informed my examination of ADR is the welcome increase in private and voluntary dispute resolution services. This has brought in its train a growing expertise in the processes themselves as well as in the training and conduct of those who act as neutrals between disputing parties. 'Alternatives' independent of the courts are gradually becoming better established; and there is no phenomenon more instructive in the formulation of public policy than an evolving market.

I intimated just now a fourth factor with a bearing on the consideration of ADR. It is a factor which has gained a certain prominence recently - which may have led to expectations that I would mention it at the head of my list. It is, of course, the rising costs of legal aid. While I do not intend today to deliver another homily on this pivotal issue, no consideration of suggested change can ignore the legal aid or other financial consequences. It would indeed be Wonderland if we could reach out for the perfect system irrespective of cost. No well-managed business can do so, and no government, as steward of taxpayers' money, can do so either. The proposition that ADR is cheaper and quicker than litigation, and therefore might effect substantial savings, including legal aid savings, must be specifically examined.

These factors present a web of opportunities and constraints which it is no mean feat to unravel. Nevertheless, I want to try to unravel them with you today, because only by doing so can we identify ways in which we may be able to secure some of the potential benefits of ADR towards a better system of civil justice than the one we have.

In order to do so, we must first remind ourselves of what it is we *want* from our civil justice system. I start from the proposition that it is a primary responsibility of good government to provide a civil justice system which maintains and advances the rule of law and furnishes the means to secure legal rights and enforce legal duties. Those means must operate impartially and must deliver compulsion, finality in the individual dispute on which judgment is given and, by association, the potential for certainty in the countless other disputes that are resolved by agreement in the shadow of the decisions handed down by the courts.

If compulsion, finality and the potential for certainty are the irreducible prerequisites of an effective civil justice system, how should they be secured? By implication, they must be secured impartially, according to law, recognising of course that the law is not immutable, but evolves, both judicially and by the will of a democratic body politic, to represent the framework of values by which collectively we choose to live.

I suggest that there is a further important requirement of a system administered by the state and financed by tax-payers (most of whom have never been and will never be involved in litigation): that it should be cost-effective.

I pause here for a moment to bring out the potential for conflict inherent in the requirements I have just identified. Procedural complexity and 'legalism' often masquerade as a necessary condition for securing impartial justice according to law. Whatever the truth on that, they both militate against cost-effectiveness. The legalism that characterises many people's perceptions of the courts has done much to nourish the view that ADR is better. But is it necessarily better in this respect? I mentioned earlier the extent to which these features now occur from time to time in both private arbitration and tribunals - both devised with the aim of providing quick, inexpensive, informal and fair remedies with the minimum of procedural complexity and legal jargon, because the courts were regarded as too formal and too remote.

Conversely, has not the small claims procedure in the County Courts demonstrated beyond doubt, for the past twenty years, that a hearing before a judge can be quick, inexpensive, informal and fair, notwithstanding that it involves the issue of legal proceedings in court?

This is a lesson that we must keep in mind in our efforts to improve our system of civil justice, especially when considering alternatives. We must use the stimulus of the demand for ADR to spur us on in these efforts. For to a large extent it seems to me that this demand is created by problems which people perceive in the current system. Rather than simply replacing current procedures with new procedures, we must continue to look into the causes of these problems and attempt to solve them. Otherwise we shall merely be papering over the cracks in our current system, rather than treating the factors which cause them.

I submit that there is nothing inherent in the nature of the judicial process that is necessarily complex; nor in the alternatives to it that is necessarily simple. If we consider embracing 'ADR' as part of our system of civil justice we must do so for other reasons, and without expectation that it will of itself cure the problems of complexity, cost and delay in the system. I would go further and say that any incorporation of ADR into the civil litigation system must be in a form which would not suffer the fate of succumbing to increasing legalism. For legalism is an enemy of efficiency and user-friendliness as well as of cost-effectiveness - whether within the judicial system or outside it.

It is incumbent on all of us who are in a position to control or influence the operation of our judicial system to do what we can to keep the law simple. Historically, conscientious draftsmen of substantive and procedural law have understandably been too often inclined to subordinate clarity to precision. Ironically, their very conscientiousness has too often led to the sacrifice of the precision they sought. The result can be a tangle of statutory provisions that are unintelligible to most of the people affected by them.

Similarly convolutions arise in procedural matters. The 1993 editions of the Supreme Court Practice and the County Court Practice together run to some five thousand pages of small print. Accessibility to the layman who wishes to establish the likely course of his or her case, or the steps to be taken in it, is virtually nil (with the exception of the procedural rules on small claims which were introduced in a far more intelligible form last October). There is a long way to go, but it is a cherished hope of mine that we shall one day reduce the size of the White and Green Books to one tenth of their present length. I believe the Commercial Court book is a superb example of this. We may need to consider different books for different jurisdictions.

I believe that there is also a need to broaden the scope of County Court arbitration and to tailor its informal rules and procedures to simple cases other than straightforward money claims. I have recently commenced public consultation on proposals for an arbitration procedure tailored to the needs of lower value personal injury claims in which complex issues of fact or law do not arise.[3] I believe that we should continue to be open to any opportunity to provide informal procedures which lay people can operate themselves without legal assistance, or with only that level of legal advice or representation essential for the speedy and efficient disposal of the case. One of the main attractions of the standard small claims procedure for litigants is the "no-costs" rule, which provides certainty as to the extent of their potential liability. Wherever possible this certainty must be maintained. Where some amount of legal representation is truly necessary, we may have to provide new schemes, such as the proposals for small personal injury claims, which allow for some costs to be recoverable. However, these costs must be categorised, relatively small and definite.

I know that the legal profession will be as aware as I am of the gradual spread of "legalism" and the problems this can cause, and I expect them to support my aims, which I do not doubt would win the appreciation of their clients. At the same time, none of us should believe that it is an easy task to achieve the necessary balance between minimising procedural complexity, and safeguarding fairness. We must also recognise that informal methods may not be appropriate to all categories of case. Some cases are inherently complex and turn on arcane points of law. Without formal procedures and the proper framework of rules such cases would take even longer to resolve than they do in the present system.

Let me sum up my argument so far. In order to identify the characteristics of ADR which are most likely to enhance our civil justice system, we must know what it is we want from that system. I have suggested that compulsion, finality and the potential for certainty are its irreducible prerequisites, and that these should be delivered according to law, impartially and cost-effectively. I have argued that legalism and procedural complexity are the enemies of cost-effectiveness, whether within the courts or outside them, and I have set out my belief that Government and the legal profession should work together in partnership to reduce these to the

[3] Published October 29, 1993.

minimum compatible with fairness. Now let us return to the characteristics of ADR to assess how they may be able to further our claims.

Unfortunately, we are not assisted in our task by the term itself. Like Humpty Dumpty, we have all tended to make ADR mean 'just what we choose it to mean', depending on our perspective. In reply to Alice's doubts about his convenient approach to the use of words, I think Humpty Dumpty hit the nail on the head when he said: 'The question is which is to be master - that's all'. To remain master of my argument, I shall resist temptations to define 'alternative dispute resolution' or to expand on the possible applications of its three constituent words. I believe our purposes will be better served if I start by acknowledging that ADR has come to denote a wide range of processes and outcomes, with an equally wide range of attributes, uses and costs. I shall then discuss their relevance to the civil justice system in the context of particular characteristics. I shall single out for closer examination arbitration, mediation and ombudsmen schemes. And the characteristics I shall touch upon in particular are whether or not a process is based in the application of law; the extent to which a solution is imposed by a third party or shaped by the disputants; whether the parties choose to submit to the process voluntarily, or are required to use it; and the relationship of the process with the civil courts.

I shall take arbitration and mediation first because both have been suggested as candidates for 'annexing' to the courts, as a means of helping litigants towards earlier settlement and so saving them time, money and stress. Members of the legal profession and others have suggested that procedural rules should be amended to encourage or require litigants, at certain trigger points in proceedings, to go to arbitration or mediation. Some proponents have suggested that the arbitration or mediation services should be those which are increasingly being offered privately, by both lawyers and non-lawyers. Others suggest that the court should provide the arbitration or mediation service itself, bringing in external arbitrators and mediators as alternatives or additions to the judicial procedure. Yet others feel that judges should themselves adopt a facilitative role at certain stages of proceedings, or in certain types of case. Most consider that legal aid should be available for these services, whichever option is adopted.

I cannot disagree with the *aim* that is common to all these suggestions. Indeed, it accords very closely with my belief that early settlement by informal means is in most instances far more satisfactory for the parties than pursuing their dispute through the courts - however user-friendly and cost-effective court procedures may be. But if the acceptance of any of these options is to secure the 'value for money' benefits of which it is capable - and secure them for the citizens who are both customers and providers of the system - we must first understand several interlocking, and to some extent contradictory, implications.

These implications differ according to whether we are talking about arbitration - which determines legal rights and liabilities by applying the law to the facts, and is binding, subject only to very limited rights of appeal to the courts; or about mediation - which is non-binding and facilitative, so that the parties' preferences, desires and circumstances are as instrumental in reaching a settlement, and as critical to shaping it, as their legal rights and duties towards each other.

The most significant difference between the two processes centres around the argument that mediation to be most effective must be voluntary. Arbitration, on the other hand, is not necessarily less effective where it is compulsory, for example in small claims proceedings or as a result of a contract clause requiring the parties to use it. One question we must consider, therefore, is whether a court-annexed system of arbitration or mediation would need to remain voluntary or whether there are arguments for *requiring* litigants to use it - as a condition, perhaps, of proceeding to a judicial hearing.

Turning first to mediation, let us consider some of the arguments. There is a widespread belief, supported by some research studies, that non-binding mediation is more likely to secure a lasting solution where the parties have chosen to use it. By doing so, they have already overcome the first hurdle towards resolving their dispute by demonstrating a preparedness to settle it informally. That suggests that, if we want a court-annexed mediation scheme to secure a high settlement rate, there should be no compulsion to use the scheme. But it might then be argued that there should be no responsibility on the part of the taxpayer to fund such a scheme, when it already funds the judicial process to which the parties may have recourse if the mediation fails. More perplexingly, what then would be the advantage of annexing a voluntary mediation scheme to the courts, or to the court process, if the scheme were not funded or (by implication) administered by the courts, and if no one were under any compulsion to use it? Indeed, some commentators have argued, persuasively in my view, that the further mediation is separated from the courts the more successful the process is likely to be. It would be unfortunate in the extreme if, in our fervour to provide a more user-friendly and effective process, we were to crush the very characteristics that made it effective.

Turning the argument round, if mediation were to be funded by the state to achieve certain purposes, should not the state be entitled to stipulate the circumstances in which the service would be used in order to realise those purposes? I leave this question open for the moment.

Let me take another aspect of the mediation dilemma. Three models of mediation have been proposed for 'annexing' to the courts. One envisages that a lawyer would act as mediator, plying between the parties to establish the *legal* strengths and weaknesses of their respective cases. By alerting each to the weaknesses, as the mediator sees them, the parties would be more likely, it is argued, to agree to settle before they reach the door of the court.

The dilemma I have with this model concerns its preoccupation with the *legal* arguments. On the one hand, this feature relates the process closely to what the courts are there to do: it might be said to assist the judicial process by weeding out weaker cases before they proceed too far, so saving the parties, and the system, money. On the other hand, I have some difficulty with the concept of an independent mediator effectively second-guessing the judge, on the same issues, without the safeguards that court procedures are designed to provide. If we build in those safeguards, we have a process which duplicates the court. If we go further and pay for the process too (either directly by training and remunerating the mediator, or indirectly by making legal aid available to eligible parties) the cases which do not settle will be publicly funded twice over. If the process is voluntary, the proportion of successful mediations may be higher, but can we guarantee that it will be high enough to offset the additional cost of the unsuccessful ones? Even taking an eighty per cent success-rate, which has been claimed for some voluntary mediation schemes, I am bound to ask: 'eighty per cent of what?' Of the caseload currently attracted to the courts, or of a higher volume of cases which might be expected to be attracted to a publicly funded mediation service?

A second model of mediation that has been suggested to me, and one which overcomes the problems associated with 'second-guessing' the judge, is for judges themselves to adopt a mediatory role. This would entail formalising the role that I know some judges already practise - that of adopting a mediatory or conciliatory role in the course of proceedings. It is quite widely claimed among the judiciary that much formal court time can be saved, with consequential savings to the parties of time, money and stress, if the judge takes the opportunity, at a pre-trial review or at other stages, to direct the parties' attention to the main issues in question and encourage sensible settlement. This is fine as far as it goes, and I have no wish to discourage an effective practice within the bounds of the necessary judicial impartiality which every member of the judiciary will be acutely anxious to preserve. However, taking this process too far might undermine the perception of judicial impartiality.

If we weigh all these factors in the balance, we begin to expose the difficulties inherent in devising a system of mediation which offers clear benefits without attracting the risks, which I have described, both to the taxpayer and to the integrity of the civil justice system. One way of preserving judicial impartiality might be to appoint a different judge for the informal mediatory process from the one who will try the case if mediation fails, or who will try other aspects of the case. This may bring advantages in terms of user-satisfaction and cost savings where the process is successful; but, unless the process is compulsory and binding, and *precludes* further recourse to the court, it does not dispose of the questions I have raised in respect of other models of mediation. There are, in addition, clear logistical problems in the requirement to provide for the potential two judges for every case.

The third model of mediation is one which expressly broadens the issues beyond the legal strengths and weaknesses of the parties' case. It expressly explores solutions which are not available to the court. For example, a business might agree to forgo its strict legal rights in favour of a solution which secured a long term supply contract at favourable rates; or a neighbour might forgo monetary compensation for a damaged tree-root in favour of an open invitation to swim in the new pool whose foundations had damaged the tree.

I see far more potential for 'user-satisfaction' in this model than in the other, for the very reason that it seeks out *new* solutions which the courts cannot provide. But for that very reason, and because it relies on the abrogation of legal rights, it is difficult to reconcile this model with the objectives of a civil justice system designed to provide compulsion, finality and certainty according to law. There may be circumstances where the value of mediation in re-establishing communication between the parties in a continuing relationship outweighs these factors, and we must consider carefully the extent to which the courts, or the procedures which govern access to them, might assist in the development of this process.

One further point on mediation, whether annexed to the court process or entirely separate from it. Mediation is in some ways as much an umbrella term as ADR, in that it describes a process comprising a range of components, some of which are optional. We might ask, for example, which of the various components of the mediation process give rise to the claimed benefits of simplicity, clarity and low cost? Is it simply the bringing together of the parties in an informal way, to discuss the issues between them? Is it the fact that neither party is compelled to attend, and that by attendance they therefore demonstrate, each to the other, a willingness to resolve the dispute? Is it the presence of their advisors, who may otherwise conduct their case only through adversarial correspondence? Or is it the presence of the neutral facilitator who may perform various functions - clarifying the issues, providing an impartial view or simply a listening ear? I have been told of a process known as "shuttle mediation" where the mediator acts as go-between to the parties, who may not be brought together in one place at all. These issues are as difficult to unravel as any in the ADR debate. But they are central to its resolution. In order to make informed decisions on the potential benefits of new processes, we must start with a good understanding of what makes them work.

I should perhaps mention in this context that I have been asked by several groups providing dispute resolution services outside the courts if my Department will participate in piloting schemes of the kind I have just described, aimed at diverting litigants from the judicial process to other informal mechanisms. Some of them have expressed surprise at my ostensible reluctance to give practical or financial support to alternative processes when I have publicly welcomed their development. I hope that what I have said today will demonstrate that I am not fundamentally opposed to such schemes and will illustrate why I have held back from espousing schemes which do not solve the dilemmas I have outlined.

Not all these arguments apply to arbitration, whatever the relationship between the process and the courts. Given that arbitration is binding, subject only to limited rights of appeal, its effectiveness is not dependent on whether the parties have chosen to use it or are compulsorily referred to it. Nor, however, is arbitration facilitative in the sense that parties are helped towards a pragmatic solution which they are free to accept or reject. Arbitration imposes a decision, in the light of the facts and according to law, in much the same way as a court does. An arbitration process annexed to the court process is for these reasons readily reconcilable with the aims of our civil justice system.

As I understand them, there are three main arguments for court-annexed arbitration. One is that a specialist in the field of a particular dispute may be better equipped to determine the dispute than a judge whose professional specialism is the law. A second is that the parties and the arbitrator are freer to specify the form and procedure adopted, providing greater potential for securing 'fitness for purpose'. A third argument asserts that arbitration is cheaper and more accessible to the man in the street.

Let us examine these arguments in the context of what is currently available through the courts. For the more complex technical cases in the High Court, there is provision for Official Referees to hear the dispute. For cases at any level of jurisdiction, there is provision for independent assessors with relevant skills and experience to assist the court at the hearing, or for the judge to refer any question to a "court expert" or "referee" for inquiry and report.

I believe that we can meet the perceived need, for technical advice or adjudication better by examining the scope for extending or adapting these existing provisions than by introducing court-annexed arbitration in the way that has been suggested. One such adaptation was in fact proposed by the Civil Justice Review in respect of the simpler housing disputes, namely, that technical assessors acting as advisors to the district judge in such cases should be remunerated from public funds. I am currently considering whether this recommendation, which was based on the results of a 1986 study, is still appropriate, bearing in mind subsequent changes to both the market and the relevant legislation.

Moving on to the arguments that court-annexed arbitration would provide flexibility of procedure, cheapness and accessibility, do we not already have an arbitration procedure integrated *within* the judicial process which provides these advantages? I refer, of course, to the County Court procedure commonly referred to as the "small claims court". County Court Rules specify that hearings under this procedure should be private and informal, and that the strict rules of evidence shall not apply. In addition, with the aim of enabling litigants to present their own case, they are assured the assistance of the district judge, and may also be represented in court by a lay person. Claims without undue complexity of a value below one thousand pounds are automatically referred into this procedure, and there is provision for the parties to cases of any value to opt for this forum or, by consent, to be referred to outside arbitrators. I believe that this model provides sufficient scope for procedural flexibility and for controlling cost and I am investigating other areas where its techniques could be applied. In my view, there is no clear case for annexing a *further* arbitration procedure to the courts; but there is certainly a case for extending the range of litigation where the parties have access to this less formal and more user-friendly forum and, as urged by the CJR, I shall continue the process of matching the forum to what is at stake between the parties wherever possible.

Our present system of private arbitration, governed as it is by the Arbitration Acts, represents a form of annexation in itself. The provisions of these Acts demonstrate a way of annexing an essentially private and consensual dispute resolution process to the courts. There is provision for the arbitrator's award to be enforced in the courts, a provision that court proceedings may be stayed where a contract in question provides that disputes should go to arbitration, and a statutory right to appeal against an arbitrator's award on grounds of misconduct or an error of law. What, then, are the arguments for further 'annexation' by requiring or encouraging parties to leave the public judicial procedure for private arbitration - whether publicly funded or not - once they have issued proceedings?

What I would call the 'funding dilemma' arises if we assume that we cannot *preclude* recourse to the courts following an alternative procedure. Even if it were possible to propose such a course of action, it could be argued, on public policy grounds, that we should not exclude the jurisdiction of the courts over disputes about legal rights and duties. This means that, whatever dispute resolution process people use outside or alongside the courts must be compatible with the aims of securing compulsion, finality and certainty, if the courts will be called upon to recognise the outcome.

At present, a high proportion of cases settle after proceedings have been issued and before any judicial hearing. Public funds are directed towards assisting settlement to the extent of applying legal aid in eligible cases, by the legal aid scheme or otherwise, to the legal costs incurred by parties in normal settlement negotiations. I referred earlier to the eighty per cent success rate claimed by some voluntary mediation schemes which are not eligible for legal aid. But what we cannot know is whether these cases would have gone on to trial, had mediation not been available. Remembering, as I remarked earlier, that these are cases where the parties have, through their willingness to mediate, demonstrated that they are open to the idea of settling the dispute informally.

It is against this background that the argument for applying legal aid to 'alternative' processes in pursuit of overall savings to the system must be considered. Taking only the disputes in which proceedings are issued, and leaving out of account the unquantifiable number of other disputes which are settled without issuing proceedings, it seems to me that in deciding to provide legal aid for the additional step of ADR for these disputes we might run the risk of increasing rather than reducing overall expenditure, unless we could be sure that the savings accruing from earlier or more frequent settlement would offset the additional cost.

Leaving aside these questions of cost, there may be a further argument against the general application of legal aid to ADR. Legal aid presupposes that the process to which it is applied is based in the application of law; it presupposes that there is a need, so undeniable that the taxpayer should support it, for legal advice or legal services relating to legal issues. What I suggested earlier was that the need seems to be *not* for further law-based processes outside the courts, given the high proportion of disputes which already settle by negotiation, and the scope we already have for securing many of the benefits of ADR *within* the evolving judicial process; but rather that the need is for processes which broaden the issues and available outcomes *beyond* those based in the law. While lawyers may *choose* to participate in such processes, either as representatives or as facilitators, the application of legal aid would suggest that their participation was a necessity. It might be argued that a system of ADR where the involvement of legal professionals was integral to successful resolution would be simply a parallel to our current system, and would thus accrue the very problems of excessive legalism and delay which underlie calls for change.

I have dwelt at some length on the various ways that have been suggested for annexing mediation or arbitration services to the courts because, as I explained earlier, this approach has attracted a strong following. I have tried to show that the arguments pose dilemmas which are not susceptible of easy answers. I have argued that, on balance, there is less of a dilemma to be resolved in developing and extending court-annexed arbitration than mediation, and that there are complex issues to resolve if we are to consider associating mediation with the civil courts. I have also explained the reasons why I do not believe it would be right to make legal aid available for ADR processes in general. I would now like to turn to another 'alternative' model for resolving disputes which has attracted less comment in the ADR debate than I believe it merits.

The concept and practice of the ombudsman, which has recently been gaining the confidence and perhaps the imagination of the public, falls into the category of processes where a solution is imposed, rather than mutually explored and shaped by the parties; but it is not confined to the resolution of disputes concerning legal rights and duties. It therefore opens up some interesting possibilities for solving the dilemmas that other models have posed.

Popularly representing justice for the small against the great - justice that is quick, inexpensive and unfettered by legalistic procedures - acceptance of the institution of ombudsman now extends well beyond central and local government administration. The concept is widely viewed as a desirable, even necessary, avenue to fairness wherever the individual is perceived to be at the mercy of an impenetrable administrative system. During the 1980s, which saw financial deregulation and growing expectations of accountability from the professions, several new ombudsman schemes were established. The Building Societies, Pensions and Legal Services Ombudsmen have statutory backing; the Insurance, Banking and Corporate Estate Agents schemes are creatures of self-regulation by their sponsoring industries.

I view the impetus behind these developments as very valuable in the field of dispute resolution between parties of unequal economic and organisational muscle. There is, however, a wide variation in the procedures and powers under which ombudsmen operate, and, until recently, no single source of information about the service they provide. I was therefore interested to learn of the establishment, a few months ago, of the Association of United Kingdom Ombudsmen with the objects of formulating and promoting standards to be met by recognised ombudsmen and of widening public awareness of recognised schemes.

A characteristic that all ombudsman schemes have in common is their potential to adjudicate between disputing parties without the trappings or expense of going to court. While in most schemes the solution is binding on the economically stronger party, within the terms of any contractual or statutory relationship between the ombudsman and the member of the scheme, the complainant does not forgo the right, where a legal remedy is likely to exist, to pursue the dispute through the courts. But in most instances where people have recourse to an ombudsman, they choose to do so because it is not important to them that the outcome should be identical to that they would achieve in court. Indeed, unlike any other adjudicatory process, it is open to the ombudsman to satisfy a sense of moral grievance rather than one of legal rights transgressed.

I make no suggestions about developing these considerations today. My aim in mentioning them is to bring the ombudsman concept and the formation of the new Association more squarely into the ADR debate. The concept certainly seems to meet a need for informal adjudication, which is final within its own terms, and which is capable of dealing effectively with disputes between parties of unequal resources - being designed to treat both parties equally irrespective of power imbalances between them. I am sure I shall not be alone in watching with interest the achievements of the new Association in disseminating information about ombudsman schemes and in securing greater procedural or jurisdictional consistency.

In this lecture I have not tried to emulate Alice's White Queen, who prided herself on her ability to believe six impossible things before breakfast. But I have tried to bring together in one lecture the range of issues which need to be considered as we continue the task of teasing out the

possible from the impossible, the feasible from the impracti-
cal and the useful from the irrelevant. I have extracted
some of the concepts which shelter under the umbrella term
ADR, and expanded on some of the questions to which I
shall need to have answers before I can move on to
considering specific changes to the current procedures in the
courts.

I now draw my lecture series to a close. As I said in my
first lecture, their purpose is to extend the knowledge of
those referred to as "the common people of the United
Kingdom of Great Britain and Northern Ireland" of the
privileges which in law and custom they enjoy in comparison with other European peoples, so that as a result of
such realisation they may appreciate their privileges and
may recognise the responsibilities attaching to them. Much
is to be said to commend the current system of justice in
this country. Reports such as the Civil Justice Review and
the Royal Commission on Criminal Justice have found the
system basically sound, though in need of important adjust-
ments. It is very valuable that this is so. I would hope that
the ordinary people in this country, when considering the
criticisms launched against the system of justice, will
remember this fact. I also hope that such criticisms as there
are will be approached in a constructive spirit, seeking to
improve rather than denigrate, to build rather than to
destroy. After some 45 years the spirit of what Miss Hamlyn
sought to produce is still important, although I would not
think it wise to aim at achieving it purely by comparison at
the expense of systems of law and justice prevailing abroad.

In my lectures I have sought to throw light on some of the
issues that face someone in my position at the moment in
relation to the administration of justice. I have tried to look
at some topics which are not often the subject of analysis
but which are, I think, interesting and of concern. I have
not, therefore, presented a comprehensive resume of my in
tray and no doubt some will be disappointed or surprised by
the fact that I have not addressed some issues which might
reasonably be thought to fall under the title of the administration of justice. In taking the approach that I have
adopted I hope that I have added a little to the knowledge
of the so-called common people of this country about

aspects of the administration of justice, and that I have also shown a little of the views that I hold on the topics that I have addressed.

Index

(All references are to page number)